CAREER BOOKS FROM WILEY

Creative Careers: Real Jobs in Glamour Fields, Blake & Bly

Dream Jobs: A Guide to Tomorrow's Top Careers, Bly & Blake

Résumés that Work, Foxman & Polsky

Getting Noticed: A Manager's Success Kit, Kravetz

High Tech Job Finder: A Guide to America's 100 Hottest Communities, Marrs & Marrs

Not Just a Secretary: Using the Job to Get Ahead, Morrow & Lebow

Flying High in Travel: A Complete Guide to Careers in the Travel Industry, Rubin

Revising Your Résumé, Schuman & Lewis

OUT ON YOUR OWN

From Corporate
to
Self-Employment

ROBERT W. BLY
GARY BLAKE

JOHN WILEY & SONS, INC.
New York • Chichester • Brisbane • Toronto • Singapore

Publisher: Stephen Kippur
Editor: Elizabeth G. Perry
Managing Editor: Katherine S. Bolster
Editing, Design & Production: G&H/SOHO, Ltd.

Library of Congress Cataloging-in-Publication Data

Bly, Robert W.
 Out on your own.

 1. Self-employed. 2. New business enterprises.
I. Blake, Gary. II. Title.
HD8036.B58 1986 658.1'141 86-15662
ISBN 0-471-01148-7
ISBN 0-471-84492-6 (pbk.)

Printed in the United States of America

86 87 10 9 8 7 6 5 4 3 2 1

To Bill Blake and Bonnie Blake-Drucker, my entrepreneurial brother and sister, with love. They guided my own entrepreneurial instincts by constantly telling me, when we were younger, to "mind my own business."

—*GB*

To Craig Wolff and Jim Sherman.

—*RWB*

— Acknowledgments —

We would like to thank our wives, Eve Blake and Amy Sprecher Bly, for reading each draft and making numerous comments and suggestions that helped us to improve the final manuscript. Special thanks to Amy for her research and editorial assistance on Chapter 8.

Thanks also to Betsy Perry, for being the best editor two authors could ask for, and to Pamela O'Connor, for her editorial contributions.

Special thanks to our good friend, Matt Burgay, who first suggested the idea of writing a book on how to venture *Out on Your Own,* and whose advice and counsel have helped us make our own ventures a success.

Contents

Introduction

Have you ever thought about how wonderful it would be to sleep as late as you want every morning?

Have you ever felt like telling your boss to "take this job and shove it"?

Have you ever fantasized about escaping from organizational life and earning a living doing exactly what you want?

If you have ever dreamed about becoming your own boss, starting your own business, and freeing yourself from the drudgery of the nine-to-five corporate world, this book is for you. *Out on Your Own* will help you assess whether the self-employed life is right for you. It will also guide you through the difficult transition from corporate employment to self-employment. This book is designed to help you cope with the social and financial adjustments, the emotional and psychological changes, and the challenges and triumphs involved in escaping from organizational life. We wrote this book to help you turn your dreams of freedom, success, and self-fulfillment into reality.

Whether you earn $9,000 a year, $85,000, or more in your present corporate job, *Out on Your Own* responds to all the questions people are asking each other in the hallways, elevators, and cafeterias of every major corporation in

1

America: How can I find a job that will reward my initiative? How can I be my own boss? How can I spend my life doing work that I find meaningful? How can I find the courage to take a chance on myself? *What does it take—and do I have what it takes—to become successfully self-employed?* This book can help you find the answers and break loose to find happiness—and more money—in your self-created career.

Out on Your Own provides a five-step process that will lead you from daydreaming about a better life to assessing what is required to succeed, then to planning your breakaway, and finally to escaping the organization and succeeding in your entrepreneurial venture.

Here are the five key steps:

Dreaming. We begin by examining how people fantasize about escaping the organization and becoming their own bosses. This section will reveal both the rewards and the problems and pitfalls of the life you dream of, and it will help you compare your dreams of success with reality.

Assessing the Options for Escape. This section will help you determine whether leaving the corporation is the right move for you or whether you would be better off staying in your job and trying to improve your life *within* the organization. We will take a look at the various escape routes from corporate life. They include starting a business, consulting, freelancing, and working for a small company. We will also discuss the potential effects of your self-employment on your friends, family, finances, and self-esteem.

Getting Ready to Escape. Here you will receive specific instructions and advice on planning your escape from corporate life. Topics include deciding whether to work at home or rent an office, whether to go it alone or take a partner, and whether to become a generalist or a specialist.

Escape! This section will lead you through the difficult transition period from the final weeks before resigning to quitting day to the uncertain first few months of self-employ-

ment. It will show you how to resign without burning your bridges behind you, how to handle financial difficulties, how to put your contacts to work and keep in touch with your former co-workers and colleagues, and how to gain visibility for your new venture.

Life After Escape. We will show you how to succeed and prosper as well as enjoy your new career or business venture. This section blends psychological advice with nuts-and-bolts information on a wide range of topics from finding clients or customers to raising your fees to monitoring your progress.

If you are like most people who work for someone else, the idea of working for yourself is tantalizing. *Out on Your Own* will help you evaluate the daydreams and see whether they should remain dreams or be turned into plans and actions that will lead to a new, different, and better way of life. If you want to escape the organization, this book can point the way. But the rest, of course, is up to you.

Good luck!

*Set me a task in which I can put something of myself,
and it is a task no longer; it is a joy; it is art.*

—Bliss Carman

PART
I

Dreaming

1

Thinking About Escaping

WHY ARE YOU THINKING ABOUT ESCAPING?

You are looking at this book because you know that many people have successfully left organizational life and found greater prosperity and happiness in self-directed careers. You have taken a look ahead, and perhaps you cannot bear the thought of twenty-five more years of waking up early, buttering up the boss, and worrying about what your superiors think of you. You need independence, autonomy, growth, and you are willing to take a few risks to get them. You value your security and safety, but you also know that self-fulfillment—working at a job you enjoy and creating something of your own—is important. You suspect that if you could create a business you enjoyed, you would be willing to make certain sacrifices to build it up. Because it would be *yours*. Because you alone would reap the profits of your labors. Because you would be working for your own prosperity, not to add to the corporation's wealth.

Do you yearn for flexibility, privacy, action, freedom? Or do you appreciate the regularity of the office, the way it keeps you in line, the way it pulls you together?

For some of us, personal happiness is obscured by the idea of just maintaining the status quo; we forget that we have the power to stop being miserable. To eliminate the misery, we must recognize our unhappiness and label if honestly. If we are not really willing to leave an unsatisfactory job, we are griping, not growing. If the dissatisfaction has become greater than the sense of security, it is time to understand precisely why the organization is dissatisfying and then to carefully plan a viable escape route from its environs.

Let's start by getting in touch with why many people are unhappy in organizational life. If you see yourself in these descriptions, you have just come to your first realization: *You are unhappy.* And you owe it to yourself, as well as to your family and friends, to change that.

1. *You are at a dead end.* You have gone about as far as you can go in the organization. There is little left to shoot for. Even a raise and a promotion would, in your mind, be too little too late. The corporate structure has no sudden surprises in store that could dynamically change your work life, your fortunes, or your ability to show a whole new side of your talents.

2. *You are bored.* Your work life has become predictable. You do the same things every day with the same people. The minutes drag by like hours. You are rarely given the opportunity to spread your wings and show how you would handle new responsibilities. You are starved for new challenges.

3. *You are not rewarded for initiative.* We all learn the meaning of fairness early in life. The American Dream stands on the idea of rewards commensurate with initiative. But you see people with less talent, less ambition, and less initiative getting ahead all the time. Why? Because they play corporate politics better than you do, cover their tracks well, or have friends in high places. Says a consultant in Stamford, Connecticut: "I saw others being advanced, and I got the message: no promotion. Now that I am out of the corporate

world, I see what a game it is—waiting for other people to recognize you, to pin medals on your chest."

Many companies give raises across the board, but you know that everyone in your department is not equally deserving. You see lip service being paid to the merit system. It is easy to feel victimized by a huge corporate superstructure. A training director at a Fortune 500 company comments: "We are being taken over, and that means that everyone is sweating his job. You are told to freeze hiring, to stop worthy projects, not to initiate new projects until the company taking over can figure out what to do with you. I feel totally powerless. All my efforts are now going to be evaluated by total strangers who have only one thing on their minds: saving money."

4. *You are envious.* Entrepreneurial success has been emphasized, praised, and publicized during the past decade. Every day we read about fortunes being made in everything from chocolate chips to microchips. The success is sweet because, usually, it is founded on the passion of a single person. You may know people who have started their own businesses and made them succeed. Although you may not have been there during the moments of anxiety when the fledgling businesses were on the brink of folding, you now see those friends looking forward to a lifetime of joy, autonomy, and prosperity.

5. *You hate your boss.* In a January 1984 *Psychology Today* article, "The Intolerable Boss," fifty-four out of seventy-three highly successful executives in large industrial companies said they had had at least one "intolerable" boss during their careers. They described these bosses as "a living snake" or "a pathological liar [whose] decisions were based on whoever talked to him last." Some people are uncomfortable with all authority figures; others understand when a boss has managerial talent and when he or she does not. When your boss is arbitrary, moody, noncommittal, or unimaginative, you may feel like quitting on the spot. But you

hold yourself back. Perhaps the boss will change. Perhaps he or she will retire or move to another department or die. In reality, these things do not often happen, no matter how much you wish them. Your boss is probably there to stay.

6. *You do not have a sense of accomplishment.* One of the joys denied people in corporate life is the ability to see a project through from beginning to end. A baker bakes cookies and sells them, performing or overseeing the whole process. So does the film director who plans, shoots, and then markets a film. But many people in corporations are stuck doing one thing all the time. At a New York insurance company, one department does nothing but respond to letters from clients around the country. One of the people in the department told us:

> *Every day I answer the same kinds of requests from our policyholders. Pretty soon, I run out of ways to say the same old thing. In fact, because the same things are written every day, the company has developed fifty-six boiler plate paragraphs we can insert. These paragraphs save us the trouble of reformulating the same thoughts every day. Unfortunately, now we have become so addicted to using these paragraphs, it has gotten so we don't have to use our brains anymore.*

Often, the people who write these letters never find out whether the problems they have addressed in their responses ever did get solved. The requests are frequently handled piecemeal, and any empathy the employee may have built up in trying to be of help to a single individual is lost.

7. *Your work does not reflect your interests or values.* Many people take a job for the wrong reasons—for security, for high pay, to fill in, or to keep busy. They rarely ask themselves the key questions: Does my job make me happy? Am I interested in what I do? Does my work reflect my values? Do I have a knack for what I do? If I were suddenly to become so wealthy that I did not have to work, would I stay on the job anyway? Or would I quit? If only your last answer was yes,

why not start planning to quit *right now?* Life is too short to spend fantasizing about what you would really like to do.

We know an accountant who longs to be in show business but who works for a hospital in the Bronx. He is young, personable, and knows the lyrics to every show tune written in the past twenty years. So what is he doing in the accounting department of a Bronx hospital? Good question. There is a clear separation between his work and nonwork activities, but he does not have the self-confidence needed to quit his job. He could get closer to his dream by utilizing his accounting skills with an entertainment company, but he will not do that either. His wife would love to see him change careers or at least change jobs. But he was a dreamer at twenty-five, he is one at thirty-five, and he will be one at forty-five.

How About You?

Have we just painted your portrait, the portrait of a person poised for change? If we have, you are taking the first step toward escaping the corporation. You still are not ready to assess the changes you would like to make, and you are probably still far from planning the escape. Now you are just dreaming about the joys—and the fears—of leaving. You may be dissatisfied, but you are not sure that you are ready to make such a big change. If more than two or three reasons for corporate blues applied to you, you may be unhappier than you think!

So now let's dream a little about how your life would change if you left your job and gained autonomy.

THE JOYS OF AUTONOMY

People who work for themselves make piles of money, live like kings, sleep till noon, drive luxury cars, summer in exotic places, fly around the country in private jets, sell their

business empires at age thirty, retire as millionaires, and live happily ever after.

Well, maybe a few of them do.

But the truth is: There are pros and cons to being on your own. It is a mistake to assume that life will automatically get better after you quit your job. Things *can* improve dramatically, but it takes patience, planning, and hard work to make a dream of success come true.

The one advantage people most often associate with being your own boss is *freedom*. After all, corporate life is full of restraints: company policies, rules, regulations, paper work, job descriptions, compensation guidelines, departmental edicts, office politics, and of course, the whims and wishes of your boss. The self-employed individual, on the other hand, answers to no one's rules but his or her own.

"That is freedom!" you say. Yet, while being your own boss solves those problems, it creates problems, too. For instance, if you are an independent consultant in a one-person practice, you will often have to work extremely long hours to meet tight deadlines and handle rush projects. Your corporate counterpart goes home at six o'clock on Friday, but you may have to work the whole weekend. If you do not put in the extra time, you could lose the account.

Of course, you are free *not* to do the work if you do not mind losing the account. However, if you need to keep your clients, you will have to give them a little emergency service every now and then. So, although you are, in theory, free to do what you want to do, the demands of the marketplace constrain you, and you have to put in those extra hours. This is not as bad as working late because the boss tells you to, perhaps; but it is not total freedom, either.

Still, when we interviewed dozens of self-employed people who had made the transition from the corporate environment, all of them placed autonomy high on the list of reasons to work for yourself. Here are a few of the things they judged best about being independent.

Freedom from the Tyranny of a Boss

"There's something to be said for not having to report to one boss who has total power over your life," says Richard Armstrong, an advertising copywriter who left his agency job to become a free-lancer. "Employed people are caught in situations where other people control their lives. I am never in that situation because I can just walk away from it. I may lose the account, but losing an account, even a big one, is not going to end my career."

Both the corporate manager and the self-employed person are accountable to others. The difference is that the free-lancer's self-respect and career satisfaction do not depend on the whims of a single individual.

"I don't have to answer to any one boss," says graphic artist Steve Brown. "If an account isn't working out or isn't worth the time, or if the people are giving me friction, I can dump them." But if your *boss* is giving you friction, you either grin and bear it, fight back, or change jobs.

Freedom to Work at Home

Working at home has a number of advantages. First, you are spared the expense of renting a separate office, and you can even deduct part of your rent or mortgage as a business expense. Second, most people work more productively in comfortable surroundings. A recent study by the Buffalo Organization for Social and Technical Innovation showed that a comfortable office environment creates an extra $1,600 of productivity annually for professionals and managers. And what office could be more comfortable than your home? Third, you save a tremendous amount of time by not dressing up for work and not commuting to the office.

"On bad days, I accomplish only twice what I did at the agency," says David Powers, a former ad agency executive who now runs his own advertising business from his home.

"I pad about the house in my favorite slippers, and when I pause from my work to look out the window, I see grass and trees instead of skyscrapers. And I've cut my commuting time from two hours to two seconds!"

Freedom from Boredom

When you are bored at work, there isn't much you can do about it. If you do not have enough to do, you can only hope your boss will realize your potential and give you more.

If you do not like what you are doing, you will probably have to change departments or, more likely, companies to find work that interests you. But self-employed people are rarely bored. They are doing the work they like best. If they do get bored, they can always take on new projects or accounts, expand into a new product or service, or even start a new company. No boss can force them to work on something that does not hold their interest.

Variety

If variety is the spice of life, corporate life can be a very bland existence indeed. Many managers find themselves stuck in narrow niches where they perform the same routine chores day in and day out. "The corporate anthill has great specialization built in," observes Jack Reid, founder of Divmet, a New Jersey manufacturing firm, "whereas with a small company you have got to be a generalist. You may have fifteen to twenty balls up in the air at one time, and you have to learn to handle it—and handle it darn well!"

If you like to be part of a team, manage small pieces of large projects, and avoid the unexpected, the corporation is for you. But if you prefer to try many new and different tasks, make quick decisions, see numerous projects through to completion, and then go on to other things, you will probably enjoy working on your own.

Activity

Many managers are dissatisfied with the slow pace at which their big companies plod along. We spoke with one salesman who said he was starting his own firm, not for the money, but because there was not enough action in being district sales manager. A small business gives this manager the freedom to create a work environment in which he will be kept busy doing the sales work he enjoys. In the corporation, he is held back by the level of work the company thinks he can handle. In his own business, the only limits that circumscribe his accomplishments are his own talent and energy.

Control

Self-employed individuals control more than their own workloads; they also supervise their business futures. "You have total control of whether you work or don't work, how much money you make, how hard you work, when you work, where you work," says Milt Pierce, a successful writer. Take your income, for example. In the corporation, your income is *not* directly proportional to your contribution to the firm. The best people in a department may work twice as hard and twice as effectively as the goldbrickers. But they do not earn twice as much. Only a few percentage points in the annual raise mark the difference between the top and the poor performers, especially at middle and lower levels of management. But when you have your own business, you are rewarded in proportion to how hard you work and how much you accomplish. Finish five projects in a month, and you earn $5,000. Complete five more the next month, and your income jumps to $10,000. You control what you do and what you earn; it is really that simple.

"Being an entrepreneur wasn't always in my mind," admits James McManus, founder of the Marketing Corporation of America (*Inc.*, June 1983). "But being in relative control of my own destiny has always been a high priority with me. . . .

So once I realized that I wasn't going to be able to get close to what I thought was my potential [working for someone else], it was mandatory that I take the risk of starting this business."

Self-Fulfillment

Do you get satisfaction out of doing your job? Or is it only the means to put food on the table?

We believe a person should enjoy work and be fulfilled by it. When we speak with corporate managers, we find that most express discontent. They complain about the boss, co-workers, or the inability to get things done within the corporate bureaucracy. In contrast, the self-employed are enthusiastic about what they do; many are totally absorbed in their work. They find the free-lance life challenging, creative, exciting, even fun.

A stellar example of this spirit is film director Steven Spielberg, who is responsible for such hit movies as *E.T.,* *Raiders of the Lost Ark, Jaws,* and *The Color Purple.* "I dream for a living," he said in an interview with *Time* magazine (July 15, 1985). "My problem is that my imagination won't turn off. I wake up so excited that I can't eat breakfast. I've never run out of energy. . . . It's just always been there."

Some people are lucky enough to find this kind of stimulation and enjoyment within the corporation. But most do not. Most people never reach this level of self-fulfillment until they are working for themselves.

Motivation to Achieve Excellence

In the corporation, many people are involved in putting out a single product. In this situation, it is hard to see the results of your own efforts. But when you have your own business, the results are obvious. After all, a committee did not do the

work; *you* did. And that provides the motivation to do the very best job you can.

"When you are on your own, you do better work," says Richard Armstrong. "As a copywriter working for an agency, I was helping to put out the agency's product, and I got very little credit for that. Nowadays, when I put a product out, I know it is all mine. It all came from my ideas. When you are in your own business, everything you do, and everything you make in terms of income depends on the quality of what you produce."

THE PROS AND CONS OF AUTONOMY

Do the benefits of autonomy outweigh the drawbacks? Only you can decide. The list below should help you to evaluate your thoughts. As you read through the left-hand column, put a plus sign next to the benefits that appeal to you. Then read through the right-hand column, and put a minus sign next to every drawback that would be a major concern.

Count up the plus and minus signs. If there are more pluses than minuses, autonomy is important to you, and you should start thinking more seriously about escaping the organization. If the minus signs outnumber the plus signs, however, security is probably dearer to you than autonomy, and you might be happier staying where you are.

Benefits of Autonomy

() Can make more money
() Work when you please
() Work at home

() Make decisions without consulting others

Drawbacks of Autonomy

() No regular paycheck
() Longer hours
() Need to supply your own office
() No one to bounce ideas off

(continued)

() No co-workers to con-
tend with

() Flexibility of small busi-
ness

() Can take risks and reap
rewards

() Tax savings

() No boss to cater to

() Can do as you please

() Can pick your own pro-
jects

() Freedom from boredom

() Being a big fish, even if
it is in a little pond

() Loneliness

() Absence of financial
resources of a large
corporation

() Can suffer personal
financial loss if the busi-
ness fails

() No corporate perks or
benefits

() Must answer directly to
clients

() Responsible for running
a company

() Must be motivated
enough to work without
supervision

() Hectic, demanding
schedule

() Miss being in a big pond

WHAT DO YOU WANT TO BE WHEN YOU GROW UP?

People of all ages dream of doing work that has meaning. We may outgrow childhood notions of being an astronaut, cowboy, nurse, movie star, baseball player, or heart surgeon, but we never outgrow the need to do the work we like best.

At this stage, you are still thinking about what it would be like to escape your company and try something that will make you happy, comfortable, and perhaps even financially well off. But all that uncertainty can be frightening. Maybe just thinking about that makes you feel like putting down this chapter and turning on the television. Don't do it! Now is the time to ask yourself some questions. What are your goals?

How long will it take you to accomplish them? You need security, you say? So do we all. Psychologist Abraham Maslow has written that our safety needs and our security needs must precede higher aspirations. Do you have higher aspirations? Will your present job fulfill them, or will it only lead to a few bucks more, a new title, a gold watch, and a pension?

All you should do right now is acknowledge the possibility of traveling a new road. Perhaps you wanted to start a business once. Or you were going to be an actor or a tennis pro. But you scrapped the idea because you thought that pastimes such as acting or tennis were not so much occupations as recreations or that starting a business was for people who had more than enough capital to venture.

More people are starting their own businesses and going out on their own than ever before. While employment in the largest industrial companies has declined by 1.5 million jobs during the past decade, the economy as a whole has added more than 20 million new jobs, thanks mostly to new businesses formed. Last year alone, some 625,000 Americans started new business enterprises of some sort. So you see, you are not alone. A lot of people are realizing that corporate life can be a drag.

In the 1950s, the era of the organizational man, big business seemed glamorous. In the 1960s, the decade of how to succeed in business without really trying, young people still aspired to become the president of Worldwide Widgets. But then came the 1970s: recession, skyrocketing interest rates, a global oil crisis, the emergence of Japan as a tough competitor. Suddenly, big business was fraught with problems, and small, service businesses began emerging. As the recession eased and the autonomy-craving baby boomers came of age, the idea of doing your own thing started to be translated into an entrepreneurial explosion. Led by the computer whiz kids, America developed a new class of young millionaires.

At first, the idea of so many youthful millionaires made

people uncomfortable. Something about the quickness and the ease of their success frightened the older generation. But America soon embraced its new tycoons. The work ethic expanded to include such concepts as "recognizing an opportunity," "risk taking," and "serving a market." Everyone could not be like Steven Jobs, who started Apple Computer, but there were fortunes waiting to be made. People were starting ice-cream companies, public relations firms, and computer stores. Good ideas abounded: Cabbage Patch dolls, pet rocks, designer jeans, gourmet take-out food, and so on.

ORGANIZE YOUR IDEAS

Think about how you could turn an idea into a new enterprise that might take you away from the nine-to-five world that has kept your imagination in chains. Make a list of the things you love. Surely, there is something about a product or service that could be improved, something that you see but others do not. Don't worry about whether that idea will yield a job. Just remember that 80 percent of all new jobs are created by new businesses.

One idea leads to another. One food lover, while eating at a Chinese dim sum restaurant, where the food circulates through the restaurant on trolleys, conceived of the idea for an American version. The name "A Movable Feast" popped into his mind. Perhaps people would enjoy paying small amounts of money for tastes of different light foods—pâté, cheese, Caesar salad. Within a few minutes, he had conceived a new type of restaurant, a name, a manner of presentation, and a menu.

Don't be like the character played by Albert Brooks in the recent film *Lost in America*. In this movie, Brooks quits his job when he is not promoted to vice president. He decides to travel around America in a Winnebago. But after a few

How long will it take you to accomplish them? You need security, you say? So do we all. Psychologist Abraham Maslow has written that our safety needs and our security needs must precede higher aspirations. Do you have higher aspirations? Will your present job fulfill them, or will it only lead to a few bucks more, a new title, a gold watch, and a pension?

All you should do right now is acknowledge the possibility of traveling a new road. Perhaps you wanted to start a business once. Or you were going to be an actor or a tennis pro. But you scrapped the idea because you thought that pastimes such as acting or tennis were not so much occupations as recreations or that starting a business was for people who had more than enough capital to venture.

More people are starting their own businesses and going out on their own than ever before. While employment in the largest industrial companies has declined by 1.5 million jobs during the past decade, the economy as a whole has added more than 20 million new jobs, thanks mostly to new businesses formed. Last year alone, some 625,000 Americans started new business enterprises of some sort. So you see, you are not alone. A lot of people are realizing that corporate life can be a drag.

In the 1950s, the era of the organizational man, big business seemed glamorous. In the 1960s, the decade of how to succeed in business without really trying, young people still aspired to become the president of Worldwide Widgets. But then came the 1970s: recession, skyrocketing interest rates, a global oil crisis, the emergence of Japan as a tough competitor. Suddenly, big business was fraught with problems, and small, service businesses began emerging. As the recession eased and the autonomy-craving baby boomers came of age, the idea of doing your own thing started to be translated into an entrepreneurial explosion. Led by the computer whiz kids, America developed a new class of young millionaires.

At first, the idea of so many youthful millionaires made

people uncomfortable. Something about the quickness and the ease of their success frightened the older generation. But America soon embraced its new tycoons. The work ethic expanded to include such concepts as "recognizing an opportunity," "risk taking," and "serving a market." Everyone could not be like Steven Jobs, who started Apple Computer, but there were fortunes waiting to be made. People were starting ice-cream companies, public relations firms, and computer stores. Good ideas abounded: Cabbage Patch dolls, pet rocks, designer jeans, gourmet take-out food, and so on.

ORGANIZE YOUR IDEAS

Think about how you could turn an idea into a new enterprise that might take you away from the nine-to-five world that has kept your imagination in chains. Make a list of the things you love. Surely, there is something about a product or service that could be improved, something that you see but others do not. Don't worry about whether that idea will yield a job. Just remember that 80 percent of all new jobs are created by new businesses.

One idea leads to another. One food lover, while eating at a Chinese dim sum restaurant, where the food circulates through the restaurant on trolleys, conceived of the idea for an American version. The name "A Movable Feast" popped into his mind. Perhaps people would enjoy paying small amounts of money for tastes of different light foods—pâté, cheese, Caesar salad. Within a few minutes, he had conceived a new type of restaurant, a name, a manner of presentation, and a menu.

Don't be like the character played by Albert Brooks in the recent film *Lost in America*. In this movie, Brooks quits his job when he is not promoted to vice president. He decides to travel around America in a Winnebago. But after a few

misfortunes, and because he has not really thought through his plans, he winds up going back to his company and groveling for the position he once snubbed. Don't try to solve all the problems involved with your ideas in one sitting. Right now, we just want you to contemplate the ideas you have had, ideas you believe in that could, with some financial backing, succeed.

Mary Kay Ash dreamed of a line of cosmetics even though there were already dozens of product lines when she started. Last year, Mary Kay Cosmetics grossed $278 million in sales, and Mary Kay Ash's personal wealth earned her a spot on *Good Housekeeping*'s list of America's fifty wealthiest women.

Failure, as well as success, can lead to opportunities for new enterprises. When Continental Airlines went bankrupt, Paul Eckel dreamed of putting together an investment syndicate that would take it over. When the buy-out failed, thousands of potential investors were disappointed. Eckel figured out a way to tap this capital. He founded Pride Airlines.

By reading this book, you are taking the first step. You are ready to admit there may be a new life out there for you. Maybe you are registering a small protest against a particularly doltish boss, co-workers who are hard to get along with, or a commute that you have grown to hate. Now, suddenly, you are doing a bit more than just asking yourself, "Is this all there is?"

You may not have a specific product or service in mind. You may just have yourself. But that can be enough. For within you may lie possibilities you have not yet imagined. In cities throughout the United States, old, middle-aged, and young people, some on executive levels, are attending college courses and seminars that deal with changing careers. They are receiving counseling, taking tests, and reviewing career case studies. These seminars are trying to give participants an idea of the skills they have, what they want from their lives and careers, and how they should go about getting it.

In a way, that is what the first section of this book intends to do: help you explore your own ideas about your future and its possibilities. This is not the time for defeatist attitudes or groaning about the responsibilities you have. This is a time to indulge your dreams and to see how deep each one runs in your life. It is time to imagine yourself doing exactly what you want, the kind of work you would do if someone handed you a million dollars right now.

Yes, we know. You would retire. But pretty soon you would be doing something with your time. What might that something be?

PROTECTING YOUR VALUES

Now that you have spent some time organizing your ideas, let's discuss your values. Your life is certainly valuable; so are your family and your friends. But does your work have to be valuable? Or can it just be a way to earn a living?

A secure income is valuable. But there are other valuable life assets: privacy, independence, appreciation, challenge, using all your talents, autonomy, being part of the process from beginning to end, dealing with people as equals, a just and fair work environment.

So when you start to examine your values, you may decide that the things you value most are often found outside a large organizational structure. Admittedly, many people excel in their nine-to-five jobs. Their values are the values of the organization: working with other people, being part of a team, enjoying job security, continuity, familiarity, structured time, and the familial setting of a particular company or department.

Is your job just a job, or does it sustain your values? If your paycheck were temporarily suspended, or if your salary were reduced, would you carry on with what you were doing because you believed in its intrinsic value, be it personal or global?

The book *In Search of Excellence* by Thomas J. Peters and Robert H. Waterman, Jr. (Harper and Row, 1982) portrays life in some of America's best-run companies. Invariably, those companies have learned to make their employees feel they are part of the action. They make them feel needed. They make them feel like winners.

Does your company tune in on your needs and values? Think about it; then answer these questions.

1. Do you enjoy teamwork, or do you prefer to work by yourself?

2. Does your company encourage you to, or discourage you from, voicing your opinion?

3. Do you value the product or service your company sells? If the company suddenly went out of business, would you continue to work with the same product or service or in the same industry?

4. Are you comfortable in your office environment?

5. Do you think your salary provides a fair reward for your talents, labors, ideas, and initiative?

6. Do you enjoy fulfilling given assignments, or would you rather pursue your own ideas?

If your consciousness, as they said in the 1960s, has now been raised, you may be thinking, "Nothing is perfect. I may not like everything about my job, but so what? It is good enough." In that case, you may not be ready to leave the corporate structure. But if you want to change your life, want to believe in what you do, want to find work that fulfills you, it is time to start planning your escape.

Maybe you see more value in starting a consulting firm than in selling securities. Maybe you would rather sell antiques and coins than be a secretary. Maybe you would like to market your own recipe for a cookie or a casserole instead of pushing paper for a food conglomerate.

We are not Pollyannas. We know that life is not an equal opportunity employer. There certainly are more jobs in organizational life than there are openings for chocolate

chip cookie makers or orchestra leaders or playwrights. But now is the time to evaluate your talents and desires, uncover the sources of your dissatisfaction, and do something about them. Are you happy right now? If not, let's channel your energy into thoughts and actions that will help you get where you want to be.

TAKING CHARGE OF YOUR LIFE

When you are dissatisfied with the way things are going, whom do you blame? Chances are, it is someone or something other than yourself. Many people use circumstances as an excuse to avoid risk taking and change. If something goes wrong, they say "I had some bad luck" instead of "I made a mistake, but I will try to do better next time." If they miss out on a raise or promotion, they complain: "This company stinks." "My boss has it in for me." They do not face the fact that they do not *have* to work for that boss; they *choose* to do so.

If you want to improve your life, find happiness in your work, and increase your income by starting your own business, you must begin by changing your attitude. Before you turn to all those monetary and security excuses, stop a moment. Get rid of the negative corporate mind-set that says, "I am only a cog in the wheel of a great machine. The machine controls my life, and I cannot change it."

Instead, you must come to grips with six fundamental truths.

1. *You Can Control Your Fate—If You Want To*
 If you want to change your situation, you can. Thousands of people have successfully made the transition from corporate employee to free-lancer. There are unlimited opportunities, but you have to plan carefully and work hard. No one is going to tap you on the shoulder and hand you a successful business.

Dan Fylstra was disgusted with the bureaucracy of the National Aeronautics and Space Administration (NASA), for which he designed space shuttle software. He struck out on his own with only $500 in his pocket. In 1978, he began writing software for the new personal computers. Today, his most successful program, VisiCalc, is one of the best-selling software packages, with over 200,000 sold. Fylstra's software company, VisiCorp., was recently reported to be worth $125 million.

Porterfield Wilson worked in Detroit on an automobile assembly line. In 1970, he opened his own dealership. Today, he is one of the most successful car dealers in the United States, with annual gross sales of $20 million.

David Bunnell was a trade journal editor when the IBM PC was becoming the most popular microcomputer for business applications. He thought, "Why not create a magazine for users of this computer?" With a partner, he raised $150,000 and launched *PC: The Independent Guide to the IBM Personal Computer* in February 1982. It was an instant success (the first issue made a profit) and now is one of the largest and most widely read periodicals in the industry.

These entrepreneurs created their own successes. They did it without rich parents, a wealthy backer, or someone to do the work for them. They wanted to create their own careers, and they did.

2. *You Must Do It Yourself*

Because everything in the corporation is done through teamwork, you may get into the habit of leaning on others for support. As a free-lancer, however, you will be on your own. Whether your business flourishes or flounders depends on *your* skills, intelligence, talent, abilities, plans, ideas, and actions. You cannot rely on others to do things for you.

One executive-turned-entrepreneur explained it this way: "If the corporate water cooler is busted, the manager

says, 'We have a problem,' and he forms a committee to study it and to decide on the best course of action. The entrepreneur, on the other hand, rolls up his sleeves, gets out his tool kit, and fixes the cooler!"

3. *You Must Believe That You Can Succeed*

According to a recent study by Boston University's Human Resources Policy Institute, 43 percent of the work force has a "gloom-and-doom" outlook on life that hampers their performance and that of their company. *Industry Week* reports that absenteeism in the United States costs American corporations $43.3 billion a year. Every day, more than 6 million Americans don't show up for work.

This negative attitude, which is harming big business, would crush the life out of a smaller company. An entrepreneurial venture simply cannot afford to support people who give anything less than 100 percent. If you want to succeed on your own, you must have a positive attitude. You must believe in what you are doing and be enthusiastic about it *even if others are negative.* As the old saying goes, "If you think you can or you think you can't, you're right!"

4. *You Must Set Goals That Challenge You*

Writing about the characteristics of successful businesspeople in *Direct Marketing Magazine* (June, 1984), retail entrepreneur Murray Raphael observes that they "constantly set higher goals" and "avoid comfort zones." In other words, the goals you set should be within your capabilities, but they should challenge you and stretch your limits. If you set easy goals, you will not grow, improve, learn, or prosper.

A man who founded one of the larger ad agencies explained it this way: "If you reach for the stars and fail, you may still get the moon. But if you reach for a tree branch and you fall, you end up in the mud."

5. *Success Requires Hard Work*

An amazing number of would-be free-lancers tell us their main motivation for leaving the corporation is to take it easy and not work so hard. They imagine that a self-employed existence will be slow, easy paced, and leave plenty of leisure time. In reality, most entrepreneurs spend years working far beyond the nine-to-five schedule; they work evenings, weekends, holidays, whatever it takes to succeed. If you are not willing to put in overtime, self-employment is probably not for you.

6. *A Positive Attitude Can Make the Difference*

Scientific research now indicates that thinking about your goals is a healthy, productive activity that can help you achieve your goals. Richard Turbo, writing in *Success* magazine (March 1982), describes how physiologist Edmond Jacobson has shown that when a person vividly imagines running, this visualizing produces real, measurable muscle contractions, as if the person were actually running. Jacobson and other researchers now believe that vivid visualizing of an activity or situation can actually help the person achieve the desired results.

In *The Joy of Working* (Dodd, Mead, 1985), Denis Waitley and Reni L. Witt advocate visualizing, which they call *self-talk.*

> *People who enjoy working play back over and over again the times they did things right. They vividly remember small successes, the appreciative compliment, a job well-done. Particularly when faced with stress, frustration, or failure, they press an "instant replay" in their minds, bringing up these positive mental images. Such positive inner reinforcement provides optimism and opportunity to overcome the problem.*

Before he became a best-selling author, horror novelist Stephen King used to lie awake and imagine that he was a famous writer being interviewed by *Playboy* magazine.

Now he *is* famous, and he was recently the subject of a *Playboy* interview. Certainly, Stephen King's writing talent and hard work are the main reasons for his success. But is it a coincidence that the specific situation he daydreamed of so often finally came true, or is it an example of self-talk in action?

DREAMS OF SUCCESS, FEAR OF FAILURE

You are now poised for change. You are almost ready to stop dreaming about escape and start figuring out how you will do it. However, two issues remain to be discussed before we march on: success and failure.

You may be serious about escaping from the organization, but perhaps you still entertain occasional doubts when, say, a sudden household expense arises, when the car wheezes and the toaster falls apart, when your spouse gets the flu and your cat is feeling sluggish. "I'll wait," you say, "until everything is just right."

Guess what? There will never be a time when everything is just right. You will always be able to find some excuse for inaction, so make up your mind to give up that argument. After all, we would still be British colonists if John Adams and Thomas Jefferson had waited for a convenient time to draft the Declaration of Independence.

Of course, entrepreneurial risk taking could result in failure. Entrepreneurs do make mistakes. Products do fail. People attempt to expand their businesses prematurely. Companies go broke. But failure is not a permanent condition. Many entrepreneurs whose first ventures do not succeed pick themselves up and try again. There *is* life after failure.

New businesses do sometimes fail, as we have said before. In 1983, the number of failures reached the second-highest level in history (the highest rate was in 1932, at the peak of

the Great Depression). There were 33,334 business failures in 1983. What that statistic does not tell you, however, is that people bounce back. As every baseball buff knows, Babe Ruth hit 714 home runs, but Ruth also struck out more often than any other player.

If failure happens to you, you will survive it. You will march on. You will not have to go on welfare or be laughed out of town. Occasional failure is part of the normal business environment. Do not allow your fears of failure to turn you into a pessimist. The experience can, in fact, be a very positive one which ensures that your next venture will be a success.

Christopher Cerf and Victor Navasky have written an amusing book entitled *The Experts Speak.* In it, they quote so-called experts who predicted failures for people who were destined to outsmart their critics. The experts sometimes fail to take into account that people have determination and spirit that surpass mere facts.

Mike Todd, the great showman, said to Walter Winchell that the musical *Oklahoma* would be a bomb because it had "no legs, no jokes, no chance." What Todd overlooked was that *Oklahoma* was something new and did not conform to tired formulas.

Mike Levy, thirty-eight, started the successful magazine *Texas Monthly* twelve years ago. "I can remember starting *Texas Monthly,* but how can I describe constant fear? The fear of not just economic loss, but the fear of failure. The biggest reason more people do not take that entrepreneurial risk is that they can't get over the hurdle of 'God, I might fail.' "

Luck, timing, and the economy will, of course, be factors to consider in your decision to leave a secure job. But hard work and a goal you believe in are even more important. With those two attributes, the likelihood you will succeed is greatly improved. And if you do fail, belief and hard work are the things that will keep you in the running and get you back on the way to success.

RICHES BEYOND THE DREAMS OF AVARICE

Two hundred years ago, Dr. Samuel Johnson was commissioned to auction off the contents of the Anchor Brewery. At the auction, he told bidders: "We are here not to sell a parcel of boilers and vats, but the potentiality to grow rich beyond the dreams of avarice."

When your buy or start a business, that business is more to you than a financial entity that sells goods and services. It represents a new way of life and the potential to make more money than your corporate counterparts can ever hope to earn. Becoming rich is a universal fantasy. However, *rich* is a relative term. Instead of wondering whether you will become the next J. Paul Getty or Steve Jobs, ask yourself, "If I quit my job and go into business for myself, will I be able to make more than I am earning now?"

The first goal you should set as a self-employed individual is to match what you were getting paid when you worked for a company. Set a deadline—a year, two years, three years—for achieving this income level. Once you achieve it, aim higher, but be realistic. Perhaps your goal will be to beat your salary by 20 percent or to double it within five years. Can you attain this income?

The answer depends largely upon the type of business you start. Part II of this book will help you assess how much you can hope to earn in your new business venture. We talked with dozens of managers-turned-entrepreneurs in all areas of small business, everything from advertising and accounting to marketing and manufacturing to publishing and writing. And the good news is that nearly all of them have dramatically increased their earnings within a year or so of leaving the corporation.

Bob Sasha, a free-lance photographer, said it took him a year before he earned an income equal to what ABC-TV had paid him as a staff photographer. A year after that, he had doubled his corporate salary. And Bob says that as a free-

lancer, he has potential to earn much more. "Your income depends on how smart you are and how good you are at selling yourself."

Free-lance copywriter Richard Armstrong points out that regardless of whether the entrepreneur makes his fortune right away, the potential for a greatly increased income is always there, which is not true when you work for a corporation. "Generally speaking, you are going to make more as your own boss than you will working for someone else," says Armstrong, "because you are only limited by how much your business can grow. Unless you are working for a *major* corporation and you are going to be the lucky one who makes it all the way to CEO, I just don't think the employees of the business ever make as much as the owners of the business do."

There are hundreds of success stories of entrepreneurs who *have* succeeded. And many of them have done so in less than five years. Sirjang Tandon, a mechanical engineer formerly employed by Memorex and IBM, used a $7,000 company bonus to start a business in his garage in 1975. Tandon manufactured and sold magnetic recording heads used in the disc drives of personal computers. After a time, he invented a recording head that would give the disc drive the ability to store twice the usual amount of data. Today, the Tandon Corporation is worth $1.5 billion and has annual sales of over $270 million. As for Sirjang, he is planning to move into a mansion on a twenty-acre site.

Jay Erlichman had become a well-paid slave at a coin dealership. He was not even allowed to go to lunch; the company sent for sandwiches to keep people close by. Jay saw the profits that were being made and decided, after many sleepless nights, to start his own dealership. That was two years ago. Jay now looks back on his years of working for someone else as a great waste and wishes he had been able to gather his courage to leave sooner. He tripled his income during his first year on his own. Now he divides his time

between his New York and London offices because he is as good at buying and selling British coins as he is at trading American coins.

We do not subscribe to get-rich-quick schemes. And we do not believe that you have to own a Jaguar, six racehorses, and three summer homes to be a success. But don't be surprised if financial rewards are a happy by-product of your new enterprise. People who do what they enjoy tend to work hard at it, and that may result in great financial rewards. In *The New Entrepreneurs,* Don Givertz says that "there has never been a better time in U.S. history to realize an ambition of getting rich."

Hard work is certainly the main ingredient, but once in a while, luck does help. David Leiderman of David's Cookies was given an early boost when his chocolate chip cookies were judged to be the best in town by *New York* magazine. More than a hundred years earlier, in 1868, a Union general sent some dried peppers from Mexico to his brother E. McIlhenny, a grocer-wholesaler in Louisiana. Tabasco Pepper Sauce was born.

If you have talent, ideas, and a willingness to work, you should consider starting a business of your own. Will you be able to make as much as you are earning right now? Probably, but it might take a couple of years before that happens. Will you double or triple or quadruple your current salary? Well, that will take some hard work, luck, and timing, but many managers who have made the break to self-employment, including the authors of this book, have done it without too much difficulty.

One disadvantage of working on your own, of course, is not having a steady paycheck to count on. But most freelancers learn to live with that uncertainty. "You can earn a hell of a lot more money working for yourself, but you can't count on an exact income," says Steve Brown, a former magazine art director. "If you stay in the company and work your way up the ladder, you may earn less, but you'll have a

steady income. You'll make $40,000 or $50,000 a year, and you'll get a raise every year. So you're secure. Working for yourself, you could have a bum year. But you just can't worry about that." Steve says it took two years for his free-lance income to match his previous salary. Today, he is making five times more than he earned while working for the magazine.

The corporate executive is all but guaranteed his unspectacular but steady 2 or 5 or 11 percent annual salary increase. On your own, you will have no such guarantee. But you will have the very real potential of earning more than the organization can offer.

As your own boss, *you* control how much you will earn. If your efforts are successful, you will earn more. If your products and ideas catch on, you will reap the rewards. And if your book becomes a best seller or you invent the next pet rock or design the next generation of microprocessors, you *can* become wealthy beyond the dreams of avarice.

Now you are ready to take the next step: assessing the alternatives open to you after you leave the corporation.

PART II

Assessing the Options for Escape

2

Breaking Corporate Bonds

OVERCOMING YOUR DOUBTS

If you still want to escape the organization, congratulations! You are now one step closer to making that dream a reality. In this chapter, we will help you to decide whether to leave or to stay. We examine the consequences of quitting, and explore the various options open to you in the world of self-employment. And we will help you make a realistic assessment of whether you are ready to make a go of it on your own. We also look closely at your chances for success.

Obviously, you feel ready for a change. The thought of ten more years of the same old routine just doesn't appeal to you. You do not want to end up like Polly Gadsby, who, according to *The Guinness Book of World Records* (New York: Sterling Publishing Co., 1979), spent eighty-six years wrapping elastic for the same company. She started working at age nine and stayed on the same job until she died in 1932 at ninety-five.

The very act of quitting your job takes tremendous courage. Although the self-employed person is the darling of the press these days, America remains a nation of employed (not

self-employed) people. When you quit to go out on your own, you become the oddball, the only one in your apartment building, on your block, or at the club who doesn't have a "regular" job anymore. Breaking corporate bonds will bring about a major change in your life, and it may take you awhile to feel comfortable with that change. Here are some of the things that you may find most difficult to cope with.

No Real Job

Chances are that you carry with you an image from childhood of Dad, dressed for work, kissing Mom, and heading for his job each morning. But the self-employed don't necessarily wear the uniforms of the nine-to-five world or go to the same places. Many dress as they please; many work at home or nearby. Although this work is just as real and difficult as any other, *people don't see it that way.* They think, for example, that free-lancers, consultants, and others who work at home aren't really working.

As an escapee from the corporate world, you'll have to cope with this attitude not only in others but in yourself as well. Early on, you may have to battle a feeling that what you're doing is unreal, play, a fantasy. Or you may have to put up with friends and neighbors who simply don't understand that *you're at work* during the day, just like them. Said one free-lance writer: "My mother kept calling to chat during the day. I think she thought I must be lonely and bored. So I sent her a photocopy of my first $2,500 check from a client. After that, she didn't call until after business hours!"

No Place to Go

Working people are trained to get dressed, take a ride, and go to a certain place day after day. And this habit is hard to

break. Some people who get fired, for example, will continue to dress for work and ride into the city even though they have no place to go. Part of the reason might be to hide their unemployment from friends and family. But we suspect the central cause is simply the ingrained habit of traveling to a workplace year after year.

Many self-employed people who planned on working at home find it difficult to do so because the workplace habit is so strong. The trick is to discover new work habits that make you comfortable. An executive-turned-entrepreneur who runs an engineering firm from his large home in Brooklyn misses suiting up and going to work. So, every morning, he puts on a dress shirt and tie, goes outside, walks around his house, reenters through the back door, and climbs the stairs to his second-floor office. He often works through the day in his undershorts, pajama bottoms, or jeans, but he always wears dress shirt and tie.

No More Rituals

The corporation is full of rituals: Friday night beers at the local pub, Christmas parties, Secretary's Week, the annual sales meeting, the company picnic, Saturday bowling and soft-ball leagues. The day you quit, all this is suddenly wrenched away from you.

If you miss these rituals when you become self-employed, the thing to do is replace them. Plenty of substitutes are available. For example, in New York City, a group of men and women who run their own public relations firms meet for lunch on the first Wednesday of every month to discuss business, new ideas, and common problems. Across town, on the same day, fifty free-lance advertising writers have a similar get-together. Although life can be lonely when you are self-employed, it doesn't have to be if you make the effort to get together with colleagues, friends, and family.

No More Perks

Naturally, you'll miss those freebies. But you will soon get over not having them. It helps to put things in perspective: Perks are nice to have but are really small rewards compared with the potential for increased income that the self-employed life can offer. Most corporations estimate that their benefits package adds 15 to 30 percent to an employee's total compensation. So, the perks received by a $40,000-a-year assistant product manager are worth anywhere from $6,000 to $12,000. Not bad, you say, until you consider that as a self-employed professional, this manager realistically could double or triple the $40,000 within a few years after leaving the corporation.

You'll find that living without corporate benefits and perks is easy. You can purchase the vital ones—health insurance, life insurance, a retirement plan, a savings plan—and simply do without the gifts, fancy lunches, and travel discounts. You won't mind the loss of perks because the rewards of personal success in your own business—self-esteem, self-fulfillment, peace, contentment, enjoyment, fun, wealth—far outstrip the artificially controlled rewards corporations bestow on their employees.

No Workday Companions

You may drift away from your old corporate cronies as you get more involved in your new life. Working for yourself will change you. You will live a different life, have different concerns, face different challenges than your corporate counterparts do. It may become harder and harder for you to relate to people you once were close to. "You will find that you have difficulty being in a social situation with people who work for other people because all they do is sit there and complain about their boss," says John Sturm, president of

Contempo Design, a company that designs and builds trade show displays.

Will all your old friendships end? Of course not. You may lose touch with some people, but true friends won't desert you. What's more, you'll find yourself making new friends and acquaintances, mostly those also self-employed or with similar interests.

FEAR OF LEAVING THE NEST

Does thinking about quitting your job make you nervous? Then join the crowd. Practically everyone who has left organizational life for the life on the outside has experienced sour stomachs, anxiety attacks, and sleepless nights while making the decision.

That's only natural. Major changes in life are always somewhat traumatic and usually cause some stress. Whether it's asking someone to marry you, buying a home, or changing careers, just *thinking* about a major life change can cause you to experience anxiety, nervousness, even fear. But don't let your fears get in the way of actions. Worry, though unpleasant, is bearable and can sometimes even act as a catalyst that propels you to swift action and hard work. However, if your fears get out of control, they may paralyze you and destroy your chances of escaping the organization.

The key to getting your fears under control is to realize that the things you fear are not nearly as terrible as you think. Nor are they likely to occur to the degree you imagine. We all have a tendency to think of the worse-case scenario, to be pessimistic. But successful entrepreneurs and free-lancers are optimists. They anticipate success, not failure.

Here are some common fears people have about leaving the corporate nest, along with the advice on how to look at the situation more realistically.

The Fear: You'll fail.
The Reality: You probably won't.

The news media have bombarded us with statistics about small-business failures. And we quoted some of these statistics ourselves in Chapter One of this book.

When worrying about your chances for success or failure, keep these points in mind:

- According to Dun & Bradstreet, 95 percent of small-business failures are caused by poor management. Be a good manager and you dramatically reduce the risk of failure.
- Many people leap into a business without giving it much thought or planning. These are the people who fail. Analyze the market, come up with a strong idea, plan your business thoroughly, and you will improve your chances for success.
- In Chapter One, we said that failure is simply a temporary setback on the road to success. Just because things go wrong doesn't mean you can't work to improve them. Too many would-be entrepreneurs give up too early.
- The figures on small-business failures are somewhat misleading. Many small companies go out of business because the owners want to close, not because they have to.
- Not every business idea remains profitable forever. Sometimes it's smart to make your profit while you can and then move on to something else.
- Success can be measured according to yardsticks other than money. If you are happy, enjoy what you are doing, and make enough money to satisfy your material needs, you are successful. Not being a millionaire does not signify failure.

The Fear: You will ruin your résumé.
The Reality: Who cares about résumés?

Do you live your life for your résumé? Many people do. They are afraid to quit their job because it might leave a gap in their employment history, ruining an otherwise perfect résumé.

Why are we so concerned about having an impressive résumé? Perhaps it is because we were brought up to please authority figures. In school, you are rewarded for pleasing the teacher, not for being creative or original. At work, you are rewarded for pleasing the boss, not for achievement or innovation. We are conditioned to behave according to standards set by institutions and organizations, and the résumé is one of those institutions.

Are you going to live the rest of your life just to please résumé readers? Or are you going to risk tarnishing that letter-perfect document in order to make some real advances in your personal happiness and business success? So *what* if there's a gap on your résumé? Once you embrace an attitude of self-reliance, you won't care. You will know that your value is in yourself, not a piece of paper.

The Fear: You'll never be able to get a job again.
The Reality: You'll get more (and better) offers then ever before.

Once you know that your value is in yourself, not in artificial standards established by institutions and organizations, an amazing thing happens: You learn that the world knows it, too. Many corporate workers discover that once they become successfully self-employed, they receive numerous job offers from their clients and customers—and at salaries and titles far higher than they ever dreamed.

Says one manager-turned-consultant: "At least once a month, a client or prospect asks whether I'd be interested in going to work for them on a full-time basis. Salary offers have ranged from $65,000 to $95,000, which is amazing when you consider I was only earning $26,000 when I left

my job three years ago. Obviously, the skills and experiences I've gained as an independent have greatly increased my value to employers. Unfortunately, I've had to turn down all these offers because I make more money on my own!"

The Fear: Without a steady paycheck, you'll have a hard time meeting the bills.

The Reality: There may be tough times, but overall, you'll prosper.

Two free-lance writers were having lunch in a Manhattan restaurant. The first was shocked to discover that his friend had bought a house and moved to the suburbs, especially when he learned what the monthly mortgage payments were.

"I really admire you for taking the plunge," he told his friend. "If I ever committed myself to paying out that much each month, I'd have to give up free-lancing and get myself a steady job!"

Many would-be self-employed people share this writer's fear. Although many free-lancers earn substantially more than their old salaries, some do not. And no matter how successful you are, free-lance income is uneven. You may go six weeks without any income, then open your mailbox one day and pull out checks totaling $12,000.

This up-and-down cycle makes many people leery of escaping the organization. But don't be. You will learn to adjust to earnings that are sporadic rather than steady. By establishing a simple but realistic budget for business and personal expenses, you'll know what it takes to meet the bills each month, and you'll plan accordingly. In time, you won't even notice that the paychecks come in different colors, from different companies, at unpredictable times, and in varying amounts. In fact, opening the day's mail to find a check or a new assignment is one of the true delights of free-lance life.

The Fear: No one will hire you.

The Reality: Relax. You'll get plenty of work.

An advertising writer, disgusted with agency life, wanted to become a free-lancer, but fear held him back. "How will I get any assignments?" he asked us. "Who in the world is going to hire me when there are so many ad agencies available?"

This is a common fear. To an organizational employee who has been handed assignments year after year, it seems inconceivable that a person working alone can convince prospects to pay money for his or her services, advice, ideas, or products. But it *does* happen—thousands of times a day, in cities and towns across the nation. Free-lancers *do* get hired by large corporations. Small manufacturing companies *do* win government contracts.

The first time someone actually hires you or buys your product or service, you will be amazed and delighted. After a time, the amazement will go away. Fortunately, the pleasure never does.

YOUR BUSINESS IDEA

Each day, the collective population of the United States generates billions of ideas: new inventions, new businesses, new products, new ways of doing things, new things to do. Yet, precious few of these ideas ever make it to the marketplace, and of those that do, only a tiny fraction succeed.

The time has come to take a cold, critical look at your business idea to see if it is workable.

Will It Fly?

Here are some questions to ask as you evaluate your idea:

- Is there a need for your product or service?
- Is the market large enough? In other words, are there enough potential customers or clients in your area to create sufficient demand for your product?
- Do you have a means of reaching these people? For example, if you want to sell a product by mail, are there mailing lists of the kind of people you want to reach?

- Can you produce what you plan to sell? Are you physically able to manufacture the product or render the service? If you've designed a revolutionary widget, can you mass-produce it efficiently and economically?
- Is there an opportunity for repeat sales? If you offer a one-shot product or service, how will you continue to make money after all your prospects have bought it? Could you make sufficient profit by offering service, parts, and maintenance to all your customers?
- Can you expand your idea into a full line of products? People who buy books on small business, for example, are also prime prospects for seminars, newsletters, and cassette tapes on the subject.
- Do you enjoy doing the type of business you have proposed? Don't do something simply because it sounds like a moneymaker.
- Is anyone else doing what you want to do? If not, why not? Perhaps your idea is a stroke of genius that no one ever thought of. Or perhaps there is a flaw in it that you have failed to spot.
- What is the competition? Is there room in your town for one more typing service, ice-cream parlor, computer consultant, or advertising agency?
- Is your product or service superior to that of the competition? If not, what can you do to make it superior?
- Is your product advantage one that the competition can easily counter? For example, if your big advantage is low price, be aware that larger competitors could engage you in a price war, wait until you go under, and then simply raise their prices again.
- Is your product or service patented? Have you made it difficult for others to copy you?
- Do you have enough money to start this business? It is dangerous to be strapped for cash in the beginning because many unexpected expenses can come up.
- Do you have reliable suppliers? If you depend on a single

supplier for a raw material or component, you could be ruined if this supplier halts shipments to you or goes out of business.

- Is there room to grow? If you are a consultant, for example, you can work only so many hours a week for so many dollars per hour. Could you increase your earnings by hiring other consultants to work for you or by packaging your advice in the form of a course, book, pamphlet, tape, or article and selling or licensing it?
- Are there any regulations to prevent you from getting started? Will you be required to pass certain exams or acquire permits and licenses?
- Do you have the necessary skills and background to run the business? If not, how can you acquire them? Can you hire others who have the background?
- Is the industry a healthy one? Financial planning, for example, is a hot profession right now, but the air pollution control business is in a slump.
- If the business fails, can you recover all or part of your investment? For example, can you sell your equipment, raw materials, and inventory to pay your debts?
- Can you quickly gear up to handle heavy demand? Can you fill orders promptly?
- Does the product tie in with a current trend? How will you stay in business after the trend fades?
- Does the idea require resources that you simply cannot provide? Launching a new soap or shampoo, for instance, requires a minimum TV advertising budget of $1 million.
- Are you legally restricted from pursuing the business? Does your employment contract prohibit you from competing with your former employer for a specific period of time?
- Is the idea original? Be sure you are not stealing an idea that is protected by copyright or patent law.
- Is your product safe? Can you be sued if your product or service harms someone?

Will It Pay?

Before you leave the corporation, you need to figure out roughly how much money you can reasonably expect to earn each year. Your income potential will depend on the type of business you plan to start. Management consultants, for example, generally earn more than free-lance graphic artists. Lawyers charge a higher hourly rate than tax preparers. Because you can expect to be paid the going rate in your profession or industry, you will want to pick a career that pays well.

Your income potential also depends on the structure of your new business. If you wish to work alone, your income will be limited by the number of hours you can work. To go beyond this limit, you could subcontract work to others and then resell their work at a higher rate. However, there are risks involved. Before you decide to subcontract, be sure you can meet the monthly payroll.

In a manufacturing operation, your gross income is your profit per unit sold multiplied by the total number of units sold. From this, you subtract your operating expenses for the year. A realistic projection of your first year's sales can give you a quick fix on your income potential. Let's work through an example to see how the actual calculation is performed.

David Roth, a chemical engineer working for a large equipment manufacturer, has decided to quit and become an independent consultant in his specialty, the scale-up of pilot-plant processes to full-size industrial operations. David plans initially to work alone because he doesn't have the funds to justify hiring an employee. If he is successful, he will consider adding full-time or part-time staff to expand his company.

Before he takes the plunge, David wants to be sure that his income from consulting can at least match his present salary. David now earns $38,000 a year in salary and bonuses. This

does not include benefits such as health insurance, sick days, and vacation pay.

According to the *Professional Consultant,* a newsletter published by Howard L. Shenson, the average chemical consultant earns a little over $500 a day. David figures $500 a day is a reasonable fee, and this is what he plans to charge his customers. But the $500-a-day figure applies only to *billable* time—that is, directly billable to the client. This includes client meetings, consultations, research, thinking, doing calculations, preparing studies, and writing reports.

However, many activities cannot be billed to the client. For example, David will have to spend a lot of time convincing potential clients to use his services. Phone calls, meetings with prospects, letter writing, the creation of a sales brochure, and business luncheons will take a tremendous amount of unbillable time. David also will not get paid for performing such necessary tasks as bookkeeping, filing, reading mail and trade journals, going to the post office, and making photocopies.

How much time, then, can David expect to spend making money? George Seiler, who heads Profit Planning Associates in Montclair, New Jersey, says that ideally, consultants should spend 50 percent of their time working, 25 to 30 percent marketing, and the remainder in a combination of personal development and administrative chores. Personal development activities help you improve your business skills and technical knowledge of your field. They include seminars, courses, lectures, and reading professional publications.

Keep in mind, however, that Seiler's figures are for *established* consultants. David is just starting out and therefore will have to spend more time marketing himself and going after business, at least until he becomes established. Let's say his time breaks down this way: 40 percent for marketing, 40 percent on billable work, and 20 percent on administrative

tasks. If David works a five-day week, this translates into two days a week spent on billable time. At $500 a day, that's an income of $1,000 a week, or $50,000 a year if he takes a two-week vacation.

Does that sound good to you? Well, $50,000 is certainly not a bad salary. It is $12,000 a year more than David Roth currently earns. However, according to what we've outlined, this is the maximum amount David can earn unless he raises his day rate, does more billable work per week, or finds some other way to generate additional income.

But wait a minute. In his old job, David had a health insurance plan. As a self-employed person, he receives no benefits and will have to buy his own insurance. Comprehensive coverage for him and his family, including major medical, hospital, and long-term disability, costs $2,000 a year. Subtract the cost of this insurance from his earnings, and you find that his *real* income is $48,000.

David plans to work from his spare bedroom to save the cost of renting an office. But he will still incur many other expenses: postage, printing, photocopying, accountant's and lawyer's fees, office supplies, business travel, entertainment (an occasional lunch with a client or prospect), magazine subscriptions, membership dues for professional organizations, and advertising. All this will cost David $10,000 a year. Subtract this from his gross earnings, and you see that his net income before taxes is only $38,000, not a penny more than he earned at his job.

Having done this analysis, David can make a much more informed decision about leaving his job. He sees that at least initially, consulting will not bring him riches beyond the dreams of avarice. In fact, it will yield an income equal to or only slightly greater than what he now earns. David must now weigh this against the many other pros and cons involved in starting a business and make his decision accordingly.

Take time now to estimate how much money you realistically can expect to earn in your first year on you own. Go through the process step by step, as David did. Taking a careful look at your income potential is an important way of assessing whether it is worthwhile for you to escape from the corporate life. Money, of course, isn't the only consideration, but it does play a major role in most people's decisions.

Take time now to estimate how much money you realistically can expect to earn in your first year on you own. Go through the process step by step, as David did. Taking a careful look at your income potential is an important way of assessing whether it is worthwhile for you to escape from the corporate life. Money, of course, isn't the only consideration, but it does play a major role in most people's decisions.

3

Escape Routes

STARTING A SMALL BUSINESS

In 1848, gold was discovered in the hills near San Francisco. Thousands of people flocked to the area to stake their claims. The Gold Rush that followed turned into one of the greatest booms in entrepreneurial activity in U.S. history. "There's gold in them thar hills!" became the battle cry of the prospectors.

The prospectors of the Gold Rush days saw an opportunity to earn money and seized it. Some of them failed, but many really did strike it rich. In today's world, however, you cannot sit back and wait for gold to be found in California or anywhere else. You will have to start or buy a small business and then work hard at it until it produces gold of a different sort.

In Chapter Two, we discussed the importance of starting out in business with a workable idea. Now, let's talk about tailoring that basic idea to fill a niche in the larger world of business.

Filling a Niche

Rarely can a small company compete head on with a big corporation. The big corporation has more resources and

can literally overwhelm the smaller firm. The way for a small company to survive is *not* to compete, but to fill a small gap in the marketplace, a niche the larger companies have overlooked or ignored.

Let's say you design a new type of personal computer. It would be difficult for you to compete with IBM in the general business market. IBM is simply too big and too well entrenched. But if you develop a highly specialized computer system—say, one designed for use in liquor stores—you could focus on this small market and be very successful.

Here is the story of a man who started a business that filled a gap in the marketplace. He saw a need and grabbed the opportunity to fill it.

Harold Longman worked on Madison Avenue in advertising, but he wanted to run a business from his rambling old home in Weston, Connecticut. Longman knew that many busy executives did not have the time to read the important business books that are published. So he created *Executive Book Summaries,* a monthly newsletter that offers condensations and summaries of significant new books. The newsletter, which sells for $59.95 a year, has enjoyed great success and now has 25,000 subscribers.

Here is another story, but this one has an unhappy ending. It is the story of an idea that sounded good but did not work.

Hank, a cabinet maker, had a strong interest in interior design. One day, a friend asked Hank to suggest ways of rearranging the furniture in her home to give the place a fresh look. For his consulting work and physical labor (he moved the furniture), he charged $100. He figured that a lot of people would want this service and decided to turn it into a part-time business.

Unfortunately, Hank quickly discovered that the idea was unprofitable. To earn the $100, he often spent many back-breaking hours moving furniture back and forth while customers seemed unable to make up their minds. A $100 job might take all day, and he would only be earning $10 to $12

an hour. When he tried to raise his rates, prospective customers balked. Apparently those who could afford to pay him more could also afford to hire a licensed interior designer. Hank has gone back to building cabinets but is studying interior design at night.

Trends Provide Niches

As times change, so do trends. And trends create the sort of niches you are seeking. These are gold mines of opportunity for sharp entrepreneurs and free-lancers. Here are some of the current trends you might be able to take advantage of.

The Information Explosion. Today, one of our most valuable resources is information. This offers a golden opportunity for the self-employed because it does not take a great deal of money or manpower to create, package, and market information for profit.

For example, one entrepreneur observed that even full-time accountants could not keep up with today's fast-changing tax laws and regulations. Because of this, clients of these accountants were not taking full advantage of legal tax-saving angles and were, in fact, paying too much tax. The entrepreneur created a newsletter, *Tax Angles,* to bring the latest tax-saving tips directly to the attention of business owners and managers. Today, *Tax Angles* is one of the most successful newsletters of all time.

Consulting. There is a need for advice in almost every area of life, from planning a wedding and buying a business to landscaping a yard and choosing a college. Consultants fill this need. One we know of is in business setting up and maintaining expensive saltwater aquariums for lawyers, doctors, dentists, and other professionals with elegant offices.

Computers. There is still plenty of opportunity in the computer field. Much of the software is written by free-lancers rather than by staff programmers. The same is true of

hardware; many computers and components are designed and manufactured by small firms rather than by the giants. Computer education is also a big field. One New York consultant, known as the "Computer Tutor," helps individuals and small businesses buy the right type of system for their operation. Another consultant trains corporate secretaries in the use of Wordstar, a popular word processing program.

Working at Home. Many consulting, mail order, and service businesses are now run from people's homes. Can you provide a service or product that would be useful to the great number of people who now work out of a garage or spare bedroom?

Working Women. Over half the female population is now employed. There is a real opportunity for products and services that cater to the working woman. Shopping for clothes (especially business clothes) by mail order is more popular than ever. Frozen gourmet foods, microwave ovens, and other time-saving products and devices can also be sold by mail.

Less Leisure Time. Because women no longer stay at home to run the house, everyone—kids, husband, teenagers—must pitch in. This means leisure time is more precious, and people want to enjoy it. At the same time, many two-income families have more to spend. So, if you can create a good leisure or recreational product, it may sell well even if it is priced high.

More Older People. Because our life-span is increasing, there are more older people around than at any other time in history. Medical advances are helping them to stay healthy and active longer, and improved retirement planning is giving the senior population more money to spend. Creating products and services for older people is another potentially lucrative market.

Health Care. A major trend is the new emphasis on fitness and health. Could you create a new exercise method, diet

plan, or fitness videotape? People are also becoming more involved in their own medical care and are increasingly less willing to take a doctor's word as gospel. Products that will educate the public in medicine and health care will continue to sell well.

Yuppies. Young people today work hard, earn a lot of money, and spend it on themselves. Singles cruises, health clubs, electronic gadgets, gourmet foods, and other such items will be hungrily consumed by this market.

Entrepreneur. Another trend on the increase is the very one we are discussing here. Products and services that inform people on how to set up and maintain their own businesses and help them to run them efficiently are very much in demand.

BUYING A SMALL BUSINESS

Starting a small business is not the only route to career independence. If you do not want to start a new company from scratch, you can always buy an existing one and make it your own. This is an attractive alternative for people who feel they would enjoy running their own business but cannot come up with a new idea, product, or concept.

Reasons for Buying a Business

There are a number of advantages to buying an ongoing business.

- *Your chance for success is greater.* The failure rate among new businesses is 90 percent within ten years. But only one out of five existing companies is heading toward bankruptcy, and 85 percent of all ongoing small businesses show a profit.
- *The concept is proven.* The risk of starting a new business, especially one that is innovative, is that you do not know if

your idea is practical until you try it. When you buy a successful business, you know in advance that it can and does work because it has a good track record.

- *You will have an established clientele.* It is difficult to get people to try a new product, switch to a new supplier, or trade in a new store. When you buy an established firm, you also buy its list of clients and customers, plus the goodwill it has established with these customers over time.
- *You will have a built-in reputation.* If the business you buy has a good reputation and is well established, you can maintain it by keeping the company name and continuing to offer the level of service that has pleased customers in the past.
- *Everything is set up and ready to go.* You can literally step in and start to run your own company the day after the deal is closed. By comparison, it takes some new companies a whole year to get going. When you buy a company, you will not have to spend the first year convincing people to give your business a try.

Reasons Not to Buy

Of course, there are also disadvantages to buying a business.

- *It requires substantial capital.* You can start your own consulting or free-lance business with little more than a typewriter, a telephone, and $300 in cash. But buying even a small business usually requires anywhere from $25,000 to $150,000 or more in start-up money. Many people are uncomfortable about going into debt for that amount, and most small-business acquisitions do involve financing.
- *There may be built-in troubles.* You may end up buying problems as well as advantages. Perhaps the owner is selling because his or her three best accounts are planning to switch to another vendor. If you do not find out about it

until after the sale, you may have bought into a situation where 50 percent of the sales are gone and the business is operating at a loss instead of a profit. Or perhaps the owner has a bad reputation in the field. This may be transferred to you as the new owner, even though you do not deserve it.

You are locked into an existing concept. The business you buy is not your own creation; it was built with the imagination and ideas of another person. You will miss the chance to nurture your own idea and see it grow. You will, in effect, be the proprietor of someone else's dream. If the act of creating something new is important to you, buying another person's company may not be for you.

Finding a Business to Buy

Finding a seller is not all that difficult. Here are a number of ways to go about it.

- Write a letter to businesses you might be interested in buying. Follow up with a phone call.
- When you visit a store or an office of a business that interests you, make contact with the owner. Mention that you are looking to buy that type of business.
- Respond to business-for-sale ads in your local newspaper and industry journals. These are listed in the classifieds advertisements under "Business for Sale" or "Business Opportunity."
- Go to a business broker. These brokers specialize in matching buyers and sellers. When the deal is made, the broker gets a commission, almost always from the seller.
- Ask local vendors if they know of any businesses for sale. A liquor distributor, for example, is a good source of information on which local bars and taverns might be on the market.
- Run a classified ad stating, "Buyer seeks small business."

Briefly describe the size, type, and location of the business you want.

Once you find some companies, you need to investigate them thoroughly. Seek out the services of the people who can help you do this. At the very least, you need an accountant to review the books and financial statements and an attorney to handle the legal aspects of the deal.

Tips on Buying a Small Business

1. Get a partner; 30 percent of buyers do this to reduce the financial burden.
2. Go into a business for which you have an aptitude. Pick something you would enjoy doing, not just something you feel will make a lot of money. Self-satisfaction is the key to success in any field.
3. Ask the seller to let you work as an unpaid employee for a few weeks so that you can get a feel for the operation. Too many people buy businesses only to discover that they hate the work.
4. Make sure your spouse is in on the decision and supports it. A husband, wife, or lover who is opposed to the venture will put an added strain on you.
5. Set a date for beginning your business search and a deadline by which you will buy a business. People who do not set deadlines procrastinate and invariably end up doing nothing.
6. Have realistic expectations. Understand the business's limitations as well as its potential.
7. Do not use the seller's asking price as a starting point for negotiation. Ask yourself what this business can earn for you and what you are willing to pay for that earning potential. The price you pay should be based on the business's value to you, not the seller's needs and wants.
8. Study the lease carefully. What is the monthly rent?

When does the lease run out? Is there an option to renew? Buying a business with a bad lease (rent too high, no option to renew, no limit on rent increases) can ruin you.

9. Evaluate the location objectively. Is it good for business? Do you like the neighborhood? Is there adequate parking?

10. Make sure that the company produces quality goods or services and that it has a good reputation. Talk with some customers (be discreet) and see how they feel.

Further Reading

An excellent source of information is Arnold Goldstein's *The Complete Guide to Buying and Selling a Business* (New York: John Wiley & Sons, 1983).

FREE-LANCING AND CONSULTING

Free-lancing, consulting—the words conjure up visions of autonomy, independence. Like the Lone Ranger and many other American heroes, free-lancers and consultants solve problems within the institution but usually work outside the corporate structure.

First, let's define terms. A free-lancer renders professional services without long-term contractual obligations to any one employer. The term *free-lance* originated during the eighteenth century when lance-for-hire mercenaries were available to fight for anyone who would pay them. A consultant provides professional or expert advice. So there is some overlap in these terms. A writer or photographer may be considered a free-lancer, but a person who offers public relations or accounting services would be considered a consultant.

We will use *consultant* to refer to people who regularly sell their advice or expertise. They may work alone or as part of a consulting firm. Free-lancers usually work alone and gen-

erally perform specific tasks rather than offer advice. Free-lancers might include tax preparers, artists, photographers, writers, musicians, actors, and illustrators. Consultants may include accountants, engineers, and specialists in everything from compensation benefits to advertising.

Thousands of Americans offer services on a free-lance basis. A free-lance mover will help you relocate. A free-lance chef will help you prepare a Thanksgiving dinner. A free-lance photographer will provide the special photograph that an organization might not be able to come up with on its own.

Consulting, according to *Venture* magazine, is a $32-billion industry in the United States. There are consultants in business, industry, religion, labor, health care, nuclear physics, small business, writing skills, stress management, and diet. *Venture* estimates that there are about 20,000 consulting firms in this country and about 35,000 to 50,000 people in the profession.

The traits needed to succeed in consulting are similar to those needed by a free-lancer. Because many free-lancers and consultants are not attached to any organization, they need to constantly hustle for new work. That takes self-confidence, an ability to manage time, an awareness of the market, and talent.

Preparing to Free-lance

Before you set out on your own, talk to several successful consultants and free-lancers. Find out what motivates them, how they spend their days, and what they feel are the drawbacks of the field. Compare your experience and expertise with theirs. Ask them how they market their services. Find out what it is like when the phone is quiet for weeks at a time. But also ask them how much you can expect to earn if you succeed. Try to discern if there is a market for the type of service you would like to provide, and ask yourself how

much time, effort, and money it will take to reach that market.

Here is a checklist you can use to find out if you have what it takes to be a successful free-lancer or consultant:

- *A salable talent.* You must have talent or expertise in a particular field. This can be, and usually is, knowledge gained through on-the-job experience or talent developed during many years of work in a given field.
- *Self-confidence.* You must believe in your own knowledge and your ability to put it to use on behalf of your clients. If you are shy or self-effacing, you will have difficulty persuading potential clients to hire you.
- *A unique approach.* You must devise a fresh approach to your work, something that will set you apart from others who offer similar services, something that will appeal to prospective clients.
- *A market.* You need to identify many, many organizations or individuals who need your service and who might be willing to hire you. It is not enough for a free-lance writer, for example, to know that 20,000 magazines are published in this country. The writer must also know which ones are open to beginners, which ones will pay satisfactory rates, and which ones accept unsolicited materials.
- *Promotional ideas.* You will have to reach out to your market and let prospective clients know what you can do for them. You will learn about some of the ways of doing this later in this book. Understand from the beginning, however, that promotion is a never-ending task. You will always be on the lookout for new clients.
- *Financial resources.* In any entrepreneurial endeavor, you will need savings to fall back on. Before you leave your corporate job, try to stash away enough to see you through several months of slow business.
- *Contacts.* You may have a few contacts at places where you have worked in the past. Also, your address book may be

filled with the names of people who may know other people who might need your services. Entirely new contacts will come from your advertising, promotional letters, attendance at trade shows or conventions, and word of mouth (after you have pleased an early client or two).

Competitive rates. Free-lancers and consultants base their fees on their own experience, the length and difficulty of the assignment, and the going rate for such services in their area. Find out what other free-lancers are asking for the kind of services you intend to provide. Then decide *how* you will charge: by the project, by the hour, or by the day.

Further Reading

For a more complete discussion of consulting, including the fee structure, you may want to read the following books and periodicals:

Books

Altman, M., and R. I. Weil. *Managing Your Accounting and Consulting Practice.* New York: John Wiley & Sons, 1983.

Bly, Robert W., and Gary Blake. *Dream Jobs: A Guide to Tomorrow's Top Careers.* New York: John Wiley & Sons, 1983.

Fuchs, J. H. *Making the Most of Management Consulting Services.* New York: Amacom, 1975.

Holtz, Herman. *How to Succeed as an Independent Consultant.* New York: John Wiley & Sons, 1983.

Kelley, Robert E. *Consulting: The Complete Guide to a Profitable Career.* New York: Scribner's, 1981.

Kishel, Gregory, and Patricia Kishel. *Cashing In on the Consulting Boom.* New York: John Wiley & Sons, 1985.

Lippit, G., and R. Lipitt. *The Consulting Process in Action.* La Jolla, CA: University Associates Press, 1978.

Steele, F. *Consulting for Change.* Amherst: University of Massachusetts Press, 1975.

Periodicals

Consultants News, Kennedy and Kennedy, Inc., Templeton Road, Fitzwilliam, NH 03447. Monthly.

Commerce Business Daily, U.S. Government Printing Office, Washington, D.C. 20402. Published five days a week.

Consulting Opportunities Journal, 1629 K St., NW, Suite 520, Washington, D.C. 20006.

ALTERNATIVE CAREERS

Buying a business, starting a business, or becoming a self-employed, independent worker—these are the most popular ways of escaping the organization. But there are others. They include:

- Working for a small company
- Franchising
- Working part-time
- Job sharing
- Moonlighting
- Intrapreneuring

Working for a Small Company

If you are disgusted with the bureaucracy of big business, you might find happiness—and more freedom—by taking a job at a smaller firm. *Small* might mean anything from a mom-and-pop grocery store to a modest manufacturing firm with over a hundred employees. The significant difference is that the company is *much* smaller and *much* less structured than the firm for which you now work.

Here are some of the advantages of working for a small firm.

- You will get a chance to perform many different tasks and

handle various projects. You will not have to become a specialist in a narrowly defined area.

- There will be fewer layers of management, hence less office politics. You will probably have direct access to the president and other top-level executives.
- The work environment will be more relaxed, more casual, and friendlier than that of a large corporation.
- Small companies are usually more dynamic. They can get more done in less time because the chain of command from the workers to the decision makers is so direct.
- You have greater opportunity to make a difference. With fewer employees, the contributions of each individual become more significant.

Working for a small company can also have its disadvantages.

- You will have less privacy, less chance for anonymity. Everyone will know almost everything about everyone else.
- Small companies have less financial stability. During hard times, the owners are quick to make cutbacks and lay off employees.
- You may get fewer benefits and a lower salary than you would in a large corporation.
- You will have fewer opportunities to advance because there will be fewer departments, jobs, and levels of management.
- Your work life may be subject to the whims and idiosyncracies of one all-powerful individual, the owner.
- The world of small business is not very glamorous. You are not likely to be in the limelight here.
- Small companies often expect workers to put in very long hours with no extra pay, recognition, or other reward.

Working for a small company may be a way for you to escape the drudgery of the corporate life. But before you make the move, analyze prospective employers carefully.

Talk with their employees to find out what conditions are really like. Don't trade one set of problems for another.

Franchising

In franchising, a company (the *franchisor*) sells the rights to operate a business (the *franchise*) to an individual (the *franchisee*). The individual buying the business pays a flat fee plus an additional annual fee based on a percentage of sales. In return, the franchisor provides a complete business, ready to run. This usually includes the name, logo, reputation and image of the parent company, as well as the design of the premises, the right to sell certain products (which the franchisor usually supplies), a proven method of running the business, advertising and promotional materials, and training.

Successful franchise operations include Burger King, Carvel Ice Cream, Fleet Feet shoe stores, and Take Time exercise centers. Opportunities to buy your own franchise are plentiful; nearly 1,500 companies offer almost 500,000 franchises.

"A franchise is an excellent way to own your own business without all the headaches associated with starting a business yourself," writes William Laird Siegal in his book *Franchising* (New York: John Wiley & Sons, 1983). "The franchisor often has had several years of hard-fought experience in the business and knows from trial and error what works and what doesn't. Usually your entire plan of action will be laid out for you by the franchisor. The only thing you have to worry about is following instructions, maintaining accurate records, and keeping the royalty checks in the mail."

Another advantage is that the franchisor usually has a track record of success. According to the Commerce Department, the failure rate of franchise outlets is less than 5 percent.

One major disadvantage of franchising is the initial purchase fee, which can range from $10,000 for a lesser-known franchise to $125,000 for a Midas Muffler shop or a McDonald's restaurant.

Another drawback is that you are locked into the franchisor's system of doing business. That means you will have very little room in which to be innovative or creative. In a sense, you are not truly independent because you must, to some extent, perform to someone else's standards.

Working Part-Time

The same old nine-to-five routine, day after day, year after year, can wear a person out. Perhaps you don't find corporate life unpleasant per se; it is just that you are tired and need a break in the routine. Part-time employment may be the answer.

In the help-wanted ads, you will find opportunities for part-time jobs in almost every field. A software company may hire free-lance programmers to work by the hour. An ad agency may need an account executive two or three days a week. Most of the time, however, the income will not match your full-time wages. In that case, you can get another part-time job, or find another source of income.

Job Sharing

Two people can share the title, responsibilities, and salary of one position. Some years ago, at the University of Rochester, two English professors, a husband and wife, shared one teaching post. Each taught half of the course load, and they shared one title and one salary. Unfortunately, job-sharing opportunities are not plentiful, and it can be hard to find a qualified partner.

Moonlighting

You might consider taking a part-time job in addition to your full-time work. For example, an accountant employed by a large corporation could moonlight by preparing tax returns for individual clients. William Greene, a promotion writer for ABC-TV, moonlights as a suspense writer; he has six published novels to his credit. If you need some spice and variety to beat the corporate blues, moonlighting may be the answer. Be warned, though: Many larger corporations frown on employee moonlighting. Either obey your company's policy, or keep your moonlighting a secret.

Intrapreneuring

An *intrapreneur* acts like an entrepreneur but still works for a big company. The intrapreneur comes up with new ideas, creates new products, and builds new businesses, but does so within the corporate structure.

However, intrapreneuring poses several difficulties. For one thing, you must work for a company that provides freedom and independence. Second, if intrapreneurs have the spirit of the entrepreneur, why don't they escape the organization and go out on their own?

"Intrapreneurs realize they may need the marketing, financial, and technical resources of the company to make their ideas succeed," explains Gifford Pinchot III, author of *Intrapreneuring* (New York: Harper & Row, 1985). In an interview in the August, 1985 issue of *For Members Only,* a newsletter published by American Express, he said, "For example, if someone has an idea of how to make planes fly faster, it helps to work for an airplane manufacturer and have access to their facilities and patents."

Perhaps it does help to have the wealth and resources of a large company behind you. But then again think of the many successful inventors—including Henry Ford, Thomas Edi-

son, and the Wright Brothers—who created great companies and products without the backing or resources of a big corporation.

Another difficulty with intrapreneuring is this: How do you become one? We have yet to see a help-wanted ad seeking an intrapreneur, or a directory listing companies that actively promote intrapreneuring. So, while this may seem like a nice balance between big business and entrepreneuring, to us it seems to be more theory than reality—at least as far as helping you find a new career is concerned.

CAN YOU TOLERATE DEBT?

The entrepreneur must be willing to take certain risks, and one of those risks is borrowing money—in other words, going into debt. The willingness to take on a debt depends on the individual and his or her background and circumstances. For some people, borrowing money may conjure up a picture of impending doom. They imagine themselves running up bills, losing their possessions, and going bankrupt. For others, borrowing money is as natural as hiring an employee or writing a letter.

We cannot tell you whether or not you should borrow money. The best advice we can give you is to view going into debt in the same way you view a variety of other risks. By doing this you may be able to gain a bit of distance from the uncertainty you feel about going into debt. Also, keep in mind the fact that people spend borrowed money every day. Most homeowners, for example, share the ownership of their homes with a bank. Millions of Americans run up huge credit-card bills, which they manage to pay eventually. And relatively few people own their cars outright. Even the federal government has run up a debt of over $1 trillion!

SHOULD YOU TAKE OUT A LOAN?

You must decide early on whether you are willing to go into debt to buy or start a business—and if you are, how deep? Can you handle the financial and emotional burden of having to meet hefty loan payments each month? (Not to mention paying rent, utilities, payroll, and vendors.) If incurring a large debt would turn you into an emotional wreck, then getting a loan may not be for you.

If you can tolerate debt, however, you may want to finance your move into self-employment. Even if you have $100,000 in savings, it does not make sense to drain your account to zero in order to pay cash to start your business. There are a number of advantages to financing the move:

- If you pay cash and the incorporated business fails, you can lose your life's savings. If you finance your enterprise and it fails, the bank will foreclose on the business and sell it off at an auction. You will lose your down payment, and you will have to pay the difference between the proceeds from the auction and what you borrowed from the bank. But at least your personal savings remain intact.
- A loan allows you to keep your savings in reserve. You may need this money to pay unexpected business expenses, such as fixing a broken boiler or coping with a 10 percent price hike from your vendors. You will also need a cushion if business is slow. The more you finance, the more cash you have in reserve.
- Interest payments on your business loan are tax deductible. This substantially reduces the cost of borrowing.

Many business people get their financing through local banks or the Small Business Administration. If you are buying a business, the seller may provide financing.

But the key consideration, from an emotional and psychological viewpoint, is to know your financial needs and what it

takes to make you feel secure. Do not spend beyond the point where you feel comfortable: the stress and insecurity are not worth the advantages.

Be a risk-taker, by all means, but a realistic risker. The realist makes informed decisions based on evidence. Realistic riskers try not to be swayed by fear, anxiety, or the views of others. Realistic riskers are not always right—most managers are right only about half of the time—but they can take risks without halfheartedness and procrastination.

Realistic riskers see debt not in emotional terms but in realistic terms. How much debt is it realistic to incur? When must the debt be repaid? If you cannot repay the debt, how much jeopardy will you be placing yourself in? Some businesses cannot hope to recoup their initial expenses until three to seven years after start-up. To attempt faster repayment would be unrealistic. If you borrow funds, try to view your debt with the clear-thinking, detached view of the realistic risker.

4

Making the Final Decision

MAKING THE DECISION TO ESCAPE

So far, we have spent most of our time weighing the pros and cons of self-employment and reviewing the various career options available to you. You have read about the joys and sorrows of the entrepreneurial life, and you have evaluated your own desires and apprehensions to see if you really want to make the break from the organization and make it on your own.

If you are ready to make the transition from corporate life to career independence, go ahead and do it. Make the decision now, and commit yourself to it. Figure out approximately when you will be ready to quit your job, and mark this date on your calendar. Come up with a rough timetable that indicates when you'll be ready to start your business. Mark this date on your calendar, too.

Don't worry about the details and the steps involved yet. We will cover them in Parts III and IV. The important thing now is to make a *firm* decision.

If you are *not* ready to take the plunge, fine. Maybe you have decided that self-employment is not for you, at least

right now. But this, too, should be a conscious decision, arrived at after careful deliberation and a liberal amount of soul-searching. Do not sit by and let indecision or inertia rule your life. Perhaps you will stick with the corporation. Maybe you will start your own corporation. But whatever you choose, it should be just that—your choice. That is why coming to a decision *now* is the crucial first step.

One Time-Tested Decision-Making Technique

Whenever Benjamin Franklin had to make a tough decision, he divided a sheet of paper into two columns. He labeled the left-hand column "Pros" and the right-hand column "Cons." In the left-hand column, he wrote down all the positive aspects of the action he was considering. In the right-hand column, he wrote the negative aspects. Then he compared the columns. If the pros outweighed the cons, the decision would be yes. But if the negatives outweighed the benefits, he would decide against the project.

On page 77 is a Franklin-style sheet for you to use in weighing the pros and cons of escaping the organization. You can simply list pros and cons and add up the number of items in each column. Or you can assign a weight to each item on a scale of 1 to 5, with 5 being "very important" and 1 being "not too important." When you have assigned a weight to each item, add up your total for each column. The difference between the two sums will help you decide against escape or in favor of it.

EVALUATING THE ADVICE OF OTHERS

Listening to others is sometimes a great idea and sometimes a tragic mistake. Charles Lindbergh didn't listen to the advice of other people. If he had, he probably would never have taken the chance and flown across the Atlantic alone.

BEN FRANKLIN'S DECISION-MAKING GUIDE

Arguments in Favor of
Escaping the Organization

Arguments Against Escaping
the Organization

1. 1.

2. 2.

3. 3.

4. 4.

5. 5.

6. 6.

7. 7.

8. 8.

9. 9.

10. 10.

11. 11.

12. 12.

Total Total

But the deaf ear he turned to advice is also the reason he persisted in his wartime isolationism, even after Pearl Harbor.

When you are about to take a big step, it is natural to seek the advice of friends, colleagues, and family. These people may have a wealth of valuable experience and knowledge to share. And because they care about you, they will give it away free.

However, when you seek advice or approval, you must consider the source. Your colleagues may discourage you from quitting simply because they do not want to see you do what they themselves are afraid to do. A friend outside the corporation may have a greater degree of objectivity in this case.

In an article in *Inc.* magazine, T. W. Samuels, president of Mark Distillery in Kentucky, talked to a number of self-made millionaires and found that ten traits predominate among successful entrepreneurs.

1. Highly competitive
2. Aggressive
3. Impatient
4. Adventuresome and willing to take risks
5. Decisive
6. Action-oriented
7. Generalists (strong on the big picture, weak on the details)
8. Innovative
9. Authoritative
10. Self-confident

These are the characteristics of a person who is willing to listen to people but not ready to abdicate the final decision. If you trust your own judgment, then by all means ask others what they think. But your opinion is the one that counts.

When you are on your own, you can't turn to a mentor and expect specific advice about whether your formula for catfish

bait made from coagulated chicken blood is good enough to spend $10,000 to test-market nationally by direct mail. Why not? Because only you are in touch with the problems, the drawbacks, the possible gains of the project. Either you will have your own feelings confirmed by listening to someone else, or you will hear an opinion based on a lack of information. You must trust yourself and let others serve as sounding boards, not gurus.

You have probably already shared your entrepreneurial ideas with others. And a few people probably saw the negative side of every idea. Now, a healthy skepticism may be a good thing, but you have to separate healthy skepticism from gloom and doom. Some people are so frightened of risk and failure that they are unable to visualize success and happiness. Others get so carried away with the merits of an idea that they don't pause to study its downside.

Look for people who can help you get in touch with your own thoughts, who will comment on what they are hearing you say, who will help you crystallize the thoughts that are bubbling up in your brain, and who will reflect the feelings that they hear as you express your ideas. They will pick up on your uncertainty or doubt or joy or enthusiasm, and then they will make you aware of what they have perceived. These are the people who can be of great aid—encouragers, listeners, mentors, people who have no axes to grind.

When seeking and evaluating advice from others, first ask yourself the following questions:

1. What experience or special knowledge does this person have that makes his or her advice accurate and useful?

2. What is his or her personal stake in the outcome of my decision? How does this personal interest affect his or her ability to give objective advice?

3. How does this person feel about me? Is he or she unable to give objective advice because he or she is emotionally involved in the decision? Or do this person's feelings possibly enhance his or her advice?

4. Has this person been self-employed? What risks has he or she taken?

5. Why did I ask for this person's advice in the first place? If I did *not* ask for it, why did he or she offer it? Don't think that every bit of supposedly objective advice you receive is unbiased. Everyone's advice is filtered through his or her own needs and experiences.

Input, both facts and feelings from people close to you, provides data for your decision-making machine. When seeking anyone's advice, make sure you weigh its objectivity and importance carefully by considering the source. The movement toward self-reliance parallels your movement away from organizational life, where many decisions are made by a group, toward self-employed life, where the buck stops at your desk.

A Final Word on Decision-Making

No book or checklist can make your decision about whether or when you should escape the organization. Only you know if and when your head and heart are ready to begin that challenging journey.

Once you *do* decide to take the self-employment plunge, however, there will be many steps to take and many things to do in order to make the transition smooth and successful. Chapters Five, Six, and Seven will help you get ready for your great escape.

PART
III

Getting Ready to Escape

5

The Plans for Escape

PLANNING YOUR ESCAPE

Mentally, you may have already turned in your office key, said good-bye, and walked out the door. But physically, you are probably still on the corporate payroll, waiting for just the right moment to call it quits.

Even a small sign of leaving—Cheshire cat smiles, lots of whispered conversations, marathon phone calls, taking home one personal possession at a time—may be enough to get you fired, so guard your actions carefully. The last thing you want right now is to lose your job. Your aim is to make a smooth transition from the days of the regular paycheck to the moment when you are suddenly on your own.

There are a number of discreet steps you can take toward preparing yourself to go out on your own.

Prepare Yourself for an Attitude Change

Once you resign, the attitudes of others—not just co-workers but vendors as well—will change. After all, why should those fawning consultants and happy-go-lucky space and sales representatives buy you lunch and remember your kids' birthdays if soon you will no longer be in a position to control

a departmental budget? And don't be shocked if the rumor goes around that you have been fired. People have become cynical about resignations and may not believe that you are leaving voluntarily.

Start Saving Your Money

Try to save at least half a year's income as a cushion to protect you during the first six months of your new life.

Don't Tell Anyone You Are Leaving

Don't tell even your best friend at the company. Secrets don't stay secrets long, and if the boss hears of your plans, he or she may throw you out while you are on your coffee break. Worse yet, your boss may beg you to stay until a replacement is found, and he or she may *never* find that replacement. You may want to give a month's notice, but you should orchestrate your leave-taking carefully. Be aware that some people will feel threatened by your plans. They may think you are being disloyal, or perhaps they resent having to carry on without you. Best to keep your plans quiet for now.

Don't Be Bitter

Don't use your last few weeks to wreak revenge on your enemies. Don't even tell people off. There is no need for that. Angry as you may be at them, these people are just bit players in the cast of your work life. With the passage of time, they will seem like cardboard cutouts.

Learn, Learn, Learn

Maybe you have paid little attention to how ads are produced at your company or how the corporation pays its bills. Suddenly, the organization can become a graduate course in business. You might even take notes on the business practices you observe all around you—how employees are inter-

viewed, how meetings are run, how the reception area is set up. Jot down brand names of computer disks, disk holders, address books, calenders, printers, typesetting machines, and other office equipment. Make a list of vendors who might be of aid to you in your new venture. You may be able to parlay your good relationship with certain vendors into a willingness on their part to extend you credit toward major purchases for your business.

Use Time to Your Advantage

Coffee breaks, lunchtime, and after work—these are the times to make your plans and check your instrument panel. Don't wait until after the plane has left the runway and is heading for uncharted territory.

You can also do a number of specific tasks while you are still working full-time at your corporate job. Here are just a few of them; you will think of many others as quitting time approaches.

- Design your letterhead and business cards, or hire a graphic designer to do it for you. If you plan to work at home, go ahead and have the letterhead and cards printed. Hold off on that step, however, if you intend to rent an office. You cannot have materials printed until you know your new address and telephone number.
- Shop for the equipment you will need. Learn which retailers offer the best quality and the lowest prices. Find out when sales will be held.
- If you plan to rent an office, start looking now. This step can take a great deal of time.
- Find a lawyer and an accountant. If you want or need a business partner, now is the time to look for one.
- While keeping your plans a secret at the office, you can start talking to outsiders about your future business. Ask friends, family, and mentors for advice about taxes, equipment, and business procedures.

- Make a list of people at your organization who might be of help to you in the future—without mentioning your plans to them yet, of course. These people can provide contacts and support later on.

WRITING A FIVE-STEP BUSINESS PLAN

You may wonder why you should write a business plan for yourself. After all, you know your own business, so there is no need to write things down. It would be like talking to yourself.

That is just what we want you to do: Get in touch with your own goals for your business. A great drama critic once said that writing a review helped him discover what his true feelings were about a particular play. Sometimes when the review was completed, the critic found that he liked or disliked a play more than he had thought before setting pen to paper. This holds true for your business idea: It will be shaped by writing down your dreams and plans.

Step 1

The first step is to describe the nature of your business. Summarize what you plan to do in one succinct sentence. Here are some examples.

The Communication Workshop is a consulting firm that specializes in helping businesspeople improve their business and technical writing.

Lucullus is a deluxe restaurant in the grand European tradition, serving international cuisine and devoted to the serious diner.

Millimeter is a trade magazine aimed at helping technical professionals in the film and videotape industry.

Bon Bon is a travel agency specializing in meeting the

needs of the show business professional who travels with a large personal staff.

In essence, you should state what you will do, whom you will do it for, and what will make your business special.

Step 2

The second part of your written plan is a statement of objectives. What would you like your business to become? What would you like to get out of it? Where do you want it to be in a year? In five years? Here are some statements of objectives.

My objectives are (1) to be the leading writing consultant in America, (2) to be known for quality and originality, (3) to be sought after by banks, insurance companies, manufacturers, and service organizations, and (4) to gross $100,000 a year.

My objectives are (1) to create advertising copy for leading industries along the eastern seaboard, (2) to work at home, (3) to retire at age fifty-five, and (4) to spend two months each year writing books.

Lucullus aims at (1) gaining an international reputation for excellent cuisine, (2) being booked two weeks in advance, (3) being an in spot for power brokers and celebrities, and (4) maintaining excellent standards of food preparation, service, and presentation.

Goal-setting should not be a form of pipe dreaming; it should be long-range thinking. As Bloody Mary in *South Pacific* put it, "If you don't have a dream, how you gonna have a dream come true?"

After coming up with objectives, you may want to communicate them to your lawyer, your accountant, and others who will figure prominently in your business. We urge you to do this as a way of furthering communication among your

employees and helping to make the objectives a bit more realistic.

Step 3

Try to predict the future by studying trends that will affect your business. This is not crystal ball gazing; it is your best thinking about societal trends that may shape what you do in the coming years. Here are a few samples of trends and the way they might influence businesses.

> The increase in commercial travel will make it necessary for small travel agencies to court business travelers as well as individual vacationers. Also, the widespread use of the computer in the travel agency field will make it imperative for even small agencies to have a computer in order to gain instant access to information about current fares. Therefore, as a two-person agency, Bon Bon Travel will have to research the purchase of a computer and consider more promotions aimed at gaining the attention of business travelers.

> The Communication Workshop recognizes the boom in data processing departments, some of which have grown so large that there is now a person in each department whose sole function is to investigate useful training programs for department members. DP departments may provide a new market for consulting services because DP people must be skilled in writing, presentation, time management, and stress management.

> *Millimeter* magazine, although once focused on technical people in the fields of film and videotape, sees rich markets in the growing cable industry and in music video in particular. Perhaps in the future, more of our editorial content and covers should focus on people in the forefront of the cable revolution.

> Rob's Ribs reflects the current popularity of Tex-Mex food and plans to capitalize on this trend by offering ribs on a take-out and delivery basis.

Step 4

It is time to take inventory of your resources. That means listing your assets, both those that show up on a balance sheet and those that do not. Do you have sufficient money, equipment, and facilities to realize your goals? Can you assemble a staff with the appropriate skills and expertise to help you accomplish your business objectives? If not, can you acquire the skills you need?

Honest answers to the following questions can help you evaluate your resources and assets:

1. How much money do you have on hand? How long will it last if you hit a dry spell?

2. Do you, as the head of the business, have the skills and knowledge you need to make your business a success? If not, how can you acquire this expertise? What schooling, courses, seminars, books, cassettes, or networking techniques would help you?

3. How many key employees do you plan to have? Will you be able to find backup people who are trained and experienced enough to step in when you need extra help?

4. If you plan to increase your sales, will you need more personnel? Where will you find them? Can you start sending out feelers now? Could you prepare a few bulletin board announcements or ads to have ready when you do actually add to your staff?

5. What new profit opportunities could you explore? For example, a consultant could consider:

- Licensing his or her seminar
- Franchising
- Offering new seminars
- Presenting a public version of the seminar
- Specializing in a new market
- Establishing a telephone hot line

- Publishing a newsletter
- Producing cassette tapes
- Writing books and articles
- Presenting lectures

Step 5

The last step is to set up intermediate goals and a timetable for meeting them. For example, if one of your goals is to gross $100,000 a year, this step will help you map out precisely how you expect to accomplish it. How many projects would you have to undertake? At what fee? How many items would you have to sell? At what price?

If your goal is to send a letter to all of your prospects four times a year or generate five new clients by direct mail, you should plan the steps: (1) shop for a computer, (2) earmark a percentage of your profits to buy the computer and the printer, (3) investigate possibilities for being trained on the computer at your place of business, (4) purchase mailing lists, (5) buy the computer, (6) hire someone to input the mailing list, (7) create the sales letter, (8) buy letterhead and envelopes, and (9) send out the mailings.

Plans for Presentations

If you will be presenting your business plan to other people—potential investors, for instance—concentrate on the financial projections and take an objective look at the risks. Here are four things investors look for in a business plan.

Evidence of Customer Acceptance

You should indicate that the product or service is being used. You might begin with a broad look at the market you will serve. How big is it? How will your idea fit in? What share of the market can you hope to control? If, for example, your

dream is to open a chain of fast-food Italian restaurants, you should try to show that there is a vast market for fast food and that people are growing weary of chicken, hamburgers, and pizza. Your chain will offer gourmet pasta and sauces ready to be taken out.

Appreciation of Investors' Needs

Provide evidence that investors will be able to cash in their stock in three to seven years after making their investment. If you are showing your business plan to a bank or to venture capitalists, it will be wise to have a detailed list of start-up and operating expenses projected for the first three years. You should also indicate a break-even point.

Evidence of Focus

Concentrate your efforts on what you do best. Investors want to make sure that the best-possible management team is running the show. So your business plan should show off your credentials as they apply to the type of business you are proposing.

Proprietary Position

Try to obtain exclusive rights to a product or process. This can be in the form of a patent, copyright, or trademark. You might include evidence of these proprietary materials in your plan when you present it to investors.

If you have carefully formulated your objectives, you will be prepared to capitalize on opportunities as they arise: a sale on computers, the availability of a student to help you input a mailing list, meeting a potential investor at a party. You will also be able to anticipate needs and problems so that you are not always forced to respond to crises. Why manage by crisis when you can manage by plan? A business plan gives

you the perspective you will need to anticipate the changes you will have to make if your business is to grow and prosper.

SPECIALIST OR GENERALIST?

We are living in an age of specialization. Back in the 1950s, people bought general-interest magazines like the *Saturday Evening Post, Look, Life,* and *Time.* But today, many magazines cater to special interests: *Working Woman, PC World, Food & Wine,* and *Architectural Digest.*

Should you specialize? That depends on two things: (1) your own expertise and (2) the kind of business that starts coming your way. As often as not, your marketplace will steer your business into a specialty. One of the authors, Gary Blake, found this to be true with his consulting business.

> *When I started the Communication Workshop, I thought I would have to offer training seminars in a number of areas, not just business writing. So my first brochure mentioned courses in stress management, time management, and presentation skills—all courses that I felt I could teach and that would help me reach a wider market.*
>
> *But corporations want specialists, not all-purpose trainers. After all, Herb Cohen is identified with negotiation skills; Dorothy Sarnoff is associated with presentation skills. I soon learned to play to my strength: writing skills. And my brochure now reflects my specialization in writing.*
>
> *I would have continued teaching business writing, but I noticed a trend that started to make me even more of a specialist. Data processing departments were growing. Many departments now include a person who evaluates training for the department. Because DP people have special writing needs, I designed a course called Technical Writing for DP Professionals and started pitching it directly to DP departments.*
>
> *Since the class was unusual, and since I seemed to be a step ahead of my competitors (who were still pitching di-*

rectly to corporate managers), I was able to carve out a nice little niche. Now, my DP course yields about half of my company's total annual profits.

However, all self-employed people must be generalists in a way. After all, you have to be able to hire people, create promotions, market your product or service, organize your work, borrow money. In other words, you need a wide range of talents and skills. The broader your experience and background, the better off you will be. In our opinion, it is easier for a generalist to specialize than it is for a specialist to pick up the skills of a generalist.

Although many self-employed people are able and willing to do the diverse chores necessary to run a business, they may occasionally want to rely on specialists to make the business run smoothly. You may know how to type, for example, but that should not stop you from hiring a typist to turn out long or important documents. And although you may be able to use a personal computer, you should not hesitate to hire a computer specialist when something complex, such as setting up a mailing list/form letter merge, needs to be done.

A doctor or a lawyer in a rural area may have to open his or her practice to anyone who walks in the door. The lawyer may do little but draw up wills and settle estates. The doctor may do everything from performing surgery to treating allergies. Chances are that the marketplace, not academic training, will ultimately dictate your specialty. Everyone likes diversity, and building a certain degree of generalism into your business may help prevent you from burning out or getting stale. William Wrigley, a salesman, used to give sticks of gum away as premiums. When he found that the gum was more popular than the product he was selling, he switched to selling gum. You can probably guess the end of this story. Wrigley's customers dictated that his future was in chewing gum.

When does specialization become too esoteric? Should an antique store specialize only in pre-Columbian artifacts? Should a bookstore carry only books about the theater? Should a specialty store carry only paperweights? In New York City, there are very successful stores that carry only theater books (three, in fact), several shops that specialize in pre-Columbian artifacts, and others that sell only paperweights. But in New Hampshire, these same stores would be in big trouble.

That brings us to the consideration of location. Only you know how well a locality will take to your business. Only you know if there are enough potential customers to justify specialization. Gary Blake teaches only writing, but writing is a critical managerial skill, so he has an enormous potential market. Realistically, he knows that his market is limited by its East Coast location. His competitors on the West Coast are much more likely to find and service West Coast corporations. But that does not really matter. Even if he aimed his business solely at DP people, his market in the tristate area (New York, New Jersey, and Connecticut) can keep his business running successfully for years.

Here is how one public relations specialist described his own need to remain, as much as possible, a generalist.

> *Four years ago, I opened a public relations firm specializing in promotions for small businesses. So, essentially, I specialize in promotion, and I specialize in small business. But these labels are deceiving because I will not turn down business that comes in from Ford or IBM or Coca-Cola. For them, I will stress my corporate experience. If a small business needs a flier or a brochure on an ad, I'll write it and find someone to design it. They do not care that I work for Ford. In fact, if they knew about it, they'd probably be scared off because they would assume that I must be too expensive.*

That brings us to the key point, the one we would like to close this section with: *It does not matter whether you think of*

yourself as a specialist or as a generalist as long as you present an appropriate image to a would-be customer.

Career counselors talk about the wisdom of having a different résumé for every different job you seek. Well, self-employed people should market to each customer or group of customers as if those customers were the main market. When Gary Blake talks with DP people, he presents himself as someone with a specialty in DP writing. But if he gets a request for a time management course, he can either turn it down or tell his prospect that he has experience and expertise in time management, which he *does* have. There is nothing to prevent you from having the best of both worlds: a specialty and a lively interest in the general work that may also come to you.

One person will not feel comfortable as a jack-of-all-trades, another person will. Listen to your customers. More than anyone or anything else, they will determine just how specialized or how diversified you and your business should be.

DOING SOME HARD THINKING ABOUT COLD CASH

How much money do you think it will take to get started in a business of your own? That little? Really?

Take whatever figure you came up with, and double it. Better yet, triple it. Now you have a more realistic idea of how much cash you will need.

Most people never realistically assess how much money starting a business requires. Instead of working out a budget, they estimate the cost. And almost always, the figure they come up with is two or three times lower than the actual cost. If you are planning to leave the secure world of steady paychecks for the uncertainty of the self-employed life, doesn't it make sense to know what the costs are before you

take the plunge? We think it does. This section provides two simple worksheets that you can use to estimate how much you will need to set up your business and keep it going until it begins to turn a profit.

Estimating Operating Costs

Operating costs, even for a small company, may be much higher than you think. Postage, photocopying, printing, and office supplies alone can cost thousands of dollars a year. Some monthly expenses, such as rent or salaries, are fairly easy to estimate; you know the going rate for an office in your town or for a secretary or an administrative assistant. Get an idea of postage and entertainment costs by talking with someone in a business similar to yours. Do some detailed research to learn the cost of raw materials and other items.

Use the worksheet on page 97 to estimate monthly operating expenses. Next to each item, write down what you will have to spend each month. Add all the figures to determine your total monthly expenditure.

Monthly expenses are difficult to trim. To generate new business, you must have contact with prospects, so you cannot eliminate phone calls, travel, entertainment, or postage and mailing costs. In fact, operating expenses may be exceptionally high during your first year, when you will be spending most of your time attracting new business.

Another thing to keep in mind when thinking about money is that in addition to being able to meet start-up costs and monthly operating expenses, you should have some extra cash on hand in case of an emergency, such as the replacement of an old or worn piece of equipment.

Estimating Start-Up Costs

Start-up costs vary widely. In a service business such as consulting, the only expenses may be a telephone, a type-

Monthly Operating Expenses for:_____

(name of your business)

Payroll	_____
Outside vendors, accountants, lawyers, bookkeepers, services	_____
Rent	_____
Utilities	_____
Telephone	_____
Insurance premiums	_____
Printing and photocopies	_____
Postage	_____
Office supplies	_____
Travel	_____
Entertainment	_____
Publications: magazine subscriptions, newsletters, books, newspapers	_____
Professional dues	_____
Education: seminars, courses, lectures	_____
Advertising and promotion	_____
Equipment upkeep and maintenance	_____
Total monthly expenses	_____

writer, a letterhead, and business cards. To start a manufacturing company, on the other hand, requires the purchase of molds, machinery, and raw materials; the initial cash outlay may be thousands or tens of thousands of dollars.

We have listed some of the equipment, materials, and other items you may need to buy. To determine your start-up costs, find out the price of each item, write it down on the list, and add up the total. This gives you a ball park estimate of how much cash you will need.

Once you have arrived at a rough estimate, you will know

whether you can afford what you want or whether you will
have to revise your plans. For example, you may have to pass
on that computer or photocopier until your business starts
bringing in some money.

Start-Up Costs for:_____
(name of your business)

Office: security deposit, real estate fees,
 first month's rent _____

Office: painting and cleaning _____

Office: furniture _____

Mover's fee _____

Incorporating, filing of business
 registration papers, licenses, and legal
 fees _____

Initial accountant's fees _____

Business insurance: initial premiums _____

Office equipment:
 Telephone system _____
 Typewriters _____
 Copiers _____
 Computers _____
 Phone-answering machine _____
 Postage machine _____
 Office equipment subtotal _____

Office supplies: initial supply of paper,
 pens, paper clips, staples, envelopes,
 etc. _____

Stationery and business cards: design
 and printing _____

Other items _____

Total start-up cost _____

Attracting Venture Capital

If you do not have enough money to make a go of your business idea, you can turn to venture capitalists for assistance. A venture capitalist is a company (or sometimes an individual or partnership) that invests in promising start-up companies.

For example, a venture capital firm might give $250,000 to a small, new computer company. In exchange for this investment, the venture capital firm gains part ownership of the computer company. The percentage will depend on the amount invested and the deal the two parties have agreed upon. If the computer company flourishes, the venture capital firm's original investment can be paid back many times over. If the computer company fails, the venture capitalist loses his or her money. To attract the attention of a venture capitalist, you have to be in a business that has potential for growth. Thus, venture capitalists are likely to invest in a company developing a new type of computer chip, but they are not about to back the career of a free-lance designer.

For a free directory of venture capital companies, write to the National Association of Small Business Investment Companies, 1156 Fifteenth Street, Suite 101, Washington, D.C. 20005.

Another good list of venture capital companies is the *Annual Venture Capital Directory* published by *Venture,* 521 Fifth Avenue, New York, NY 10175, (212) 682-7373.

Venture capitalists, however, are not the only source of money. Local banks often lend money to fledgling enterprises in the community. Other ways to obtain money include:

• Taking a partner
• Seeking a personal loan from a friend or relative
• Taking out a second mortgage on your home

- Selling off some investments
- Drawing on personal savings

THE PLEASURES AND PERILS
OF PARTNERSHIP

A partner, like a spouse, can be a help or a hindrance. And you should go into a partnership the same way you would go into a marriage: with both eyes wide open. At best, a partnership is a good thing. Think of Abraham and Straus, Sears and Roebuck, Evans and Novak. But the history of partnerships has its failures, too—many, many of them.

Whether or not you choose to go into business with a partner will depend on your financial resources, your skills, and your personal and emotional needs. Let's look first at some of the reasons you might want to consider finding a partner. Then we will examine some reasons *not* to have one.

What Could a Partner Do for You?

Here are some reasons you might want a business partner.

- He or she will share the burdens of the business by doing half the work, participating in all the major decisions, and putting up half of the funds.
- A partner will provide company for you during work hours and will serve as a one-person support group.
- A partner who has skills that are different from yours may be able to manage a part of the business that you do not feel able to handle. This will allow you to go about those tasks you like best or are best suited to perform.
- He or she will provide a second source of moneymaking suggestions, many of which would never have occurred to you.

Think about some well-known partnerships in which indi-

viduals combined their talents with successful results: Proctor and Gamble, the Smith Brothers, Hewlett-Packard. The partnership of Bell and Howell serves as an excellent example of two talents making up an even stronger team. Donald Bell handled the administrative end of the business while his partner, Albert S. Howell, ran the engineering lab when they started their company in 1907.

Sometimes a partner can help even an established business. One young entrepreneur started a film and video magazine for the trade. The magazine was turning a profit, but the day-to-day operation was too much for one person to handle. The entrepreneur advertised for a partner in the *New York Times*. He found a man who became co-publisher and who turned the magazine into the industry leader. They recently sold the magazine for several million dollars, and both partners made a huge profit. You, too, may want to consider the option of joining with someone whose new business has grown too large for a single person to run.

Recognizing a good idea was at the heart of the partnership forged at the beginning of the century between Murray Spangler and William Hoover. Spangler was a janitor who swept floors at a department store in 1907. To calm a hacking cough caused by the dust, he rigged up a dustless cleaner using an electric fan motor and a pillowcase connected to a broom handle. Spangler started manufacturing his invention, but he had no money to market it—until he sold a vacuum cleaner to his cousin. Her husband, William H. Hoover, immediately recognized the invention's potential. Spangler and Hoover started making vacuum cleaners together in 1908.

Partners and Problems

As the old saying goes, "Familiarity breeds contempt." You and your partner may whirl happily through the first few

months of your business venture, carried along by the spirit of the challenge. Sooner or later, however, the honeymoon will end, and reality will reassert itself. It is at this time that the arguments begin. We know two partners in a travel agency who got along famously until the business started to sour. One partner wanted to spend money promoting the business; the other did not. The tension between them created a rift that doomed the agency.

As time goes by, you and your partner may simply begin to get on each other's nerves. You may find yourself wishing, for example, that your co-owner would not talk so much, and in such a loud voice, on the telephone, or that he or she would stop tapping pencils on the desk while you are trying to think of a new way to market your product.

Choosing a family member as a business partner is no assurance that your business life will be smooth and success-ful. It can work extremely well in some instances. Look at the Gimbel Brothers, for example. In other circumstances, such a partnership can result in a years-long feud. In alliances between relatives, agreements should be put on paper, and each party should have a lawyer.

Two brothers-in-law we know worked together on a piece of software. They signed an agreement, but one of the partners did not show the contract to a lawyer. Then a dispute erupted. The language of the agreement was so vague that the other partner was able to interpret the clause in his favor. The dispute was eventually settled, but it caused bad feelings for a long time.

Yet, the potential for problems has not stopped an increas-ing number of married couples from going into business together. According to the Internal Revenue Service, in 1977, there were 257,899 husband-and-wife teams billing about $6 billion in sales. By 1982, the number had increased 52 percent to 392,167, and sales were up to $18.9 billion. To get a perspective on family members who go into business with each other, you may want to read *How to Start a Family Business and Make It Work,* by the editors of *In Business.*

Business partners, whether they are relatives, old friends, or virtual strangers, often come close to blows when one partner acts without asking the other's advice or consent.

We know two partners who have not exchanged a word in three years. Secretaries pass notes between them. Apparently, the feud began when one partner hired his son without telling the other partner. Pretty soon, they started functioning independently, widening a rift that may never be healed.

In advertising, the word *you* is persuasive; in therapy, the word *I* can be a healthy sign; but the word that sounds sweetest in a partnership is *we*. You share the agonies and the ecstasies and try not to remind each other of how crucial *you* were to any one sale. You will find that over the years, your talents, skills, and rewards will even out.

Tips for Making a Partnership Work

Here are just a few of the ways you and your partner can solve the problems that arise in your business relationship.

- *Talk every detail out before you go into a partnership.* Partners who do not first discuss their feelings about money, debt, advertising, office supplies, relatives in the business, personal calls, and other such details are like couples who get married before discussing their feelings about having children.
- *Communication is vital.* If your partner is driving you crazy, you must let him or her know that you're upset. Don't bury your feelings, and don't expect your partner to read your mind.
- *Be kind and tactful.* Don't say, "You're screwing up the books!" Try a bit of rephrasing: "I'm not quite comfortable with the way the books are being handled. Do you think it would be better to do them this way?"
- *Try to understand your partner's personality.* Often, personality differences are a source of conflict between partners.

For some emergency help in gaining this understanding, you may want to read two books: *I'm OK—You're OK,* by Thomas Harris, and *Coping with Difficult People,* by Robert Bramson. Both books explore personality with an eye toward helping readers understand the sources of common personal conflicts.

We wish you and your partner luck, but if the partnership dissolves, at least you will know that others have gone the same route. Estrangement among business partners is increasing. The number of cases submitted to the American Arbitration Association supports this conclusion. Partnership disputes rose from 130 in 1980 to 231 in 1982.

The AAA, a nonprofit organization with 60,000 expert arbitrators, has been settling business disputes since 1926. In contracts that establish business relationships, it is common practice to insert a standard AAA clause that requires all partners to submit to binding arbitration even if only one partner seeks it. Fees to cover costs are determined on a sliding scale based on the dollar amount of the claim. The process is informal, and the decision is absolute. If the parties have an AAA clause in their contract, they are bound by AAA rules of arbitration rather than by state or local laws. AAA's main office is located at 140 West Fifty-first Street, New York, NY 10020; (212) 484–4000. There are twenty-six regional offices.

6

The Details

HOME OFFICE OR RENTED OFFICE

ONE of the genuine delights of self-employment is that, in many instances, you have the option of working in your home. Many types of businesses can be operated from your home. You can run an ad agency, a typing service, a mail order company, a catering service, a software firm, a publishing company, and dozens of other types of companies from a spare bedroom or garage. Self-employed professionals, freelancers, and artists, including editors, accountants, musicians, photographers, interior decorators, architects, and press agents, can also work at home.

There may be legal limitations, of course. Before setting up a home-based business, check with your attorney to make sure you are operating within the law. It may be perfectly legal to give piano instructions to individual students in your apartment, but it may not be legal for you to hold symphony orchestra rehearsals there.

Of course, working at home is not for everyone. In fact, in a recent survey of corporate managers, the majority said they would *not* want to work at home, even if the corporation gave them the option to do so.

105

Advantages of Working at Home

- *Casual dress.* You can dress as you please unless you expect a visit from a client.
- *Informal atmosphere.* You can do exactly as you please. You will feel more relaxed and less pressured. You can do your work without worrying how busy you appear to others.
- *Freedom of schedule.* Because your office is always nearby, you can work whenever you want to. There is no commute.
- *Saves money.* You eliminate the expense of renting an outside office. And you can deduct from your taxes a portion of your rent or mortgage and utilities.
- *Enjoyment.* Instead of working in a cold, impersonal office, you can work in familiar, comfortable surroundings. Instead of being constantly bombarded by interruptions and visitors, you can work in peace and solitude, alone with your thoughts and ideas. Plus you will be physically closer to your family and able to spend more time with them.

Disadvantages of Working at Home

Here are a few of the disadvantages you may encounter.

- *Clutter.* A home office, if allowed to expand uncontrolled, can rapidly eat up space meant for living.
- *Lack of separation from work.* A home office may not give you the separation of home and work life that you need. You may be unable to get your mind off business because you know your office is just down the hall, full of work waiting to be done.
- *Reduced status.* In some industries, potential clients or customers may look down their noses at you. This may prevent you from landing big or prestigious accounts. In advertising, for example, the big accounts go to big agen-

cies with elegant offices on Madison Avenue. Basing a
small agency in your apartment might make it tough for
you to convince prospects to hire you.

• *Problems with neighbors.* Neighbor problems come in two
forms: (1) You bother your neighbors by causing a parade
of couriers, clients, and vendors to stamp in and out of
your home. (2) Your neighbors bother you by dropping
by for coffee or a chat "since you don't work anymore." If
either form of the neighbor problem threatens to drive
you out of business, you will probably have to consider
renting an office.

• *Lack of resources.* Most office buildings are close to printers,
copy centers, restaurants, hotels, convention centers, and
other business resources. Lack of available resources can
be a problem to those who work in homes located far away
from these services.

Tips on Setting Up a Home Office

1. If possible, locate your office in a separate room far
from distractions such as the kids or a TV set.

2. If you don't have a separate room, isolate your work
space in some way. A tall bookcase or a room divider might
help.

3. Have a separate phone line for your business. After
business hours, put the office phone on an answering ma-
chine or service so that you can relax.

4. Arrange your work space so that you can get the
maximum tax benefit out of your home office. Remember,
the larger the space devoted to your office, the bigger your
deduction.

5. If you do not expect prospects or clients to visit your
home office, don't spend money on expensive furniture
unless it makes you feel more professional.

Tips on Renting an Office

1. Make sure you can afford the rent. Don't get in over your head.

2. Location is an important consideration. Choose an office convenient to services, transportation, and your clients. Make sure the neighborhood is safe enough so that people will be comfortable about coming to visit you.

3. Choose an attractive, comfortable building. Older and elegant is fine; shabby is not.

4. Find a space large enough so that there is room to expand as your business grows.

5. Make sure the terms of the lease are favorable. You should have the option to renew, and there should be a limit to how much the rent will increase.

6. Make sure there is convenient, reasonably priced parking nearby.

7. Choose a fully occupied building. A half-empty building often indicates that a neighborhood or business district is declining.

NUTS AND BOLTS: BUYING OFFICE EQUIPMENT AND FURNITURE

Although your funds may be limited right now, we suggest you equip and furnish your office as completely as possible. There are two benefits to working in a well-equipped office. First, modern business equipment makes you more productive and therefore more profitable. Second, working in a legitimate office reinforces the feeling that your business enterprise is indeed real.

Used office furniture is an economical alternative to expensive new items. Go to a secondhand office furniture dealer, or check the papers for furniture sales sponsored by companies that are redecorating, moving, or closing offices.

You may be able to find a perfectly satisfactory piece of used furniture at a fraction of its cost when new.

Telephone

Later, when your business grows, you may need to buy a sophisticated telecommunications system (available from private suppliers or the phone company). For now, however, a standard telephone is probably good enough.

Ask your phone company what inexpensive options it offers. At the least, you may want to have call waiting, conference calling, and call forwarding.

Choose your long-distance service carefully if you plan to be making numerous out-of-town calls. The advantage of selecting a smaller carrier over AT&T is lower cost; the smaller companies sometimes can reduce your long-distance bill by 10 to 50 percent. The disadvantage may be lower quality. Many people complain that calls are not always as clear as they are with AT&T. Keep asking around, though. The competitors seem to be improving with time.

Your office phone must never be unattended during business hours. For this reason, you need to obtain a phone-answering machine or hire an answering service (see the section "Phone-Answering Service" on page 116).

You can buy a reliable machine for $60 to $250. Look for these features in an answering machine.

- A remote-control device that lets you call in and get your messages when you are away from the office.
- A machine that provides sufficient time for callers to leave their messages. Sixty seconds is not long enough for some business messages.
- Changeable tapes. Because tapes can wear out, a machine with changeable tape cassettes is better than one with a built-in tape.
- A machine that lets you control the exact length of your

message. Some machines have a fixed length for your greeting, forcing you to fill the unused time with recorded music or leave an uncomfortable pause.

You should avoid the temptation to record a clever or cute greeting; such a message is unprofessional. Make yours simple, short, and to the point.

Desk and Chair

Comfort is the thing to look for when selecting an office chair. Many white-collar workers spend six hours or more each day sitting in their chairs; so it is worth paying a little extra for a chair that gives you firm support for your back and a comfortable seat. A good office chair can cost $350 or more. Buying a *used* chair can save money.

Make sure your desk has enough surface area to comfortably hold your papers as well as a telephone, computer terminal, lamp, and calculator.

File Cabinets

A good file cabinet is essential. Start with a two- or four-drawer metal unit, and buy additional cabinets as your files expand. Make sure the cabinet can accommodate hanging files. They are easy to find, whereas ordinary files can slip to the bottom of the drawer unseen. If you keep sensitive papers, order your cabinet with a lock and key.

Shelves

A couple of inexpensive bookshelves are useful for storing business and reference books, directories, files, and papers.

If you need to store product inventory, metal warehouse shelves are one answer. These shelves come unassembled, so

you can adjust them to any height. You can buy warehouse shelving from an office or warehouse supply firm.

Typewriter

At the very least, you will need a good electric typewriter for producing business correspondence, reports, and other documents. In this age of word processing and computers, businesspeople expect correspondence to be cleanly typed and error-free. Erasures, cross-outs, and overstrikes are unacceptable.

Buying a name-brand typewriter will ensure a reliable machine and service when you need it. Look for a self-correcting feature that allows you to go back and correct mistakes without having to change ribbons or use some other external correction technique. Newer electronic typewriters even have small computerlike memories in which you can store short documents such as letters, memos, and short reports.

Computer

The personal computer can dramatically increase the productivity of your business office. Used as a word processor, the computer can cut typing time in half. Changes and corrections can be made electronically, right at the computer terminal. Endless typing and retyping of multiple drafts is eliminated, saving time, effort, and operating costs.

With a spelling-checker program, you can turn your computer into an electronic proofreader that corrects most of your spelling and typing mistakes. With a mail-merge program, your computer can personalize a form letter with the customer's name and address.

A data base program allows you to store complete customer and prospect files on the computer. Using a few

simple keyboard commands, you can ask the computer to find and display any file in an instant.

A communications program, used in conjunction with a device called a *modem,* lets your computer talk to other computers over the phone. You can send and receive important business documents in seconds instead of days.

What does all this cost? A personal computer with enough power for business use costs anywhere from $1,200 to $4,000 and up. Programs cost several hundred dollars apiece. Ask other businesspeople what computer they are using. Then go to a computer store, and take a look for yourself. Tell the salesperson what your particular needs are.

As with typewriters, it may be safer to stick with a brand name than to try a new or unproven model. In personal computers, Apple and IBM are the safest bets.

Photocopier

A photocopier is a good investment for businesspeople who often need to copy office materials. The price of photocopiers has dropped dramatically in recent years. The cost of a good small-office machine can range from $900 to about $3,000.

Here are some questions to ask before you buy a copier:

- What size paper does it use? Most use 8½ by 11 and 8½ by 14. Only a few of the smaller copiers can accommodate 11 by 17.
- Does it require special paper? Some copiers can copy onto any paper, including your letterhead. Others require special copier paper that only a copier dealer or office supply firm can provide.
- Are any special chemicals required? Some models require you to change toner or handle other messy chemicals. Others use cartridges that can be changed quickly and easily.

- Does it copy on both sides of a page? This is important if you have frequent need of two-sided copies.
- What mechanism is used to feed original documents into the machine? This can determine how fast you can copy.
- How many copies can it make at one time? The limit on most machines ranges from 1 to 99 without resetting.
- What kind of service is available, and what does it cost? Copier breakdowns are frustrating, and repairs are expensive.

When shopping for a copier, take along a list of the copying jobs you will do most frequently as well as any special requirements, such as color copying, reducing or enlarging, or oversized paper. Look for a copier that can handle all of your routine copying and at least some special tasks.

MORE NUTS AND BOLTS: GETTING READY FOR THE PAPER WORK

Lasting impressions are often based on small details. Therefore, it will be worth your while to pay attention to *every* aspect of your business, right down to the color and quality of the paper on which your company letterhead is printed.

Letterhead

All business correspondence, even short, informal notes, should be typed on paper that bears your company letterhead. So one of your first moves should be to get the letterhead designed and printed.

There are two ways to do this. One is to visit a printer and select a stationery style from a catalog. This method is economical and fast. However, the selection is limited, and you may not find a design that you like or that is right for your business.

The alternative is to hire a graphic artist to design stationery for you. The price of this service can vary from $100 to $500 for the design of a letterhead, envelopes, and business cards. This fee does not include the price of printing the letterhead. If you want the designer to create a company logo for you, that will also cost extra, sometimes a great deal extra. However, a logo is not necessary for the average start-up firm.

How many envelopes and letterheads should you print? An economical number is 500 of each. If you print less, you will be paying a higher price per piece. If you print more, you may be stuck with extras if you decide to make a change in your company name or letterhead design six months to a year from now. Printing costs for 500 letterheads and envelopes could run anywhere from $100 on up.

The look and feel of the paper you use also says something about your image. If you want to impress clients, use better-grade paper, one with some body and texture. A quality paper, such as Classic Laid, has a *weave* running through it that is visible when you hold the paper up to the light. Ask your printer to show you samples.

You will also have to choose a color. White and off-white are acceptable, but some people prefer other colors to make their letters stand out. Popular colors include beige, light brown, light blue, and gray.

Business Cards and Mailing Labels

Traditionally, business cards are printed with the same design used on the letterhead. However, some people use cards employing various gimmicks, such as artwork, photographs, folds, and pop-ups. They may be printed on a wide variety of materials ranging from paper and cardboard to nylon, fiber glass, and plastic. Let your taste and judgment be your guides.

Some people use oversize cards. Their advantage is that

they stand out from other cards. Their disadvantage is that they don't fit into card cases, Rolodexes, and other storage devices.

If you will be mailing packages or large envelopes, you will need mailing labels that bear your company name, address, and telephone number. Have these printed up when you order your stationery and cards. Use the same typeface and general design, leaving plenty of room in which to type the address of the receiver. Most printers offer self-stick labels in different sizes and qualities. Ask your printer to show you some samples.

Checks

A special bank account for your company helps keep your personal finances separate from your business finances. To open a business account, take an original copy of your certificate of doing business (or any other paper to establish you as a legal business enterprise) to a commercial bank. Bring with you enough cash (or a check made out to cash) to open the account. Except for submitting your business papers, the procedure for opening the business account is the same as that for opening a personal account.

Order checks in a large ledger format rather than the pocket-size checkbook used for personal accounts. This ledger has extra space for you to keep notes about your business transactions.

Choose dignified, businesslike checks. Avoid elaborate designs with sunsets or sailboats. Checks should be printed with your company name and address as well as a box or space for you to note the nature of the transaction.

Your Company Name

The name you choose will tell people a good deal about your company. For one thing, it sets a tone and can determine the

type of clientele you will attract. The name Frank's Gym calls up the image of a sweaty, dingy training room for boxers and weight lifters. But if Frank changes the name to Omni VI Fitness Center, the image changes to one of Nautilus machines, aerobics classes, running tracks, saunas, whirlpools, health food bars, and other trappings that will draw a more affluent crowd.

The simplest way to set up a business is to file a certificate of doing business with the city clerk of your town, borough, or city hall. For a small fee, usually around $35, you file this form to establish yourself as a bona fide business. However, you must use your *own name* or a recognizable variation of it when filing this certificate. If you want to establish a firm using a made-up name or a proper name other than your own, the procedure is more complex, and you should consult your attorney.

STILL MORE NUTS AND BOLTS: HIRED HANDS

Many beginning entrepreneurs try to do everything themselves. They type their own letters, deliver reports to clients in person, do their own tax returns, and collect their own overdue bills.

It is only natural to want to do it all yourself to save money and retain control over these important areas. But it is also a mistake. By taking on too many tasks, you may spread yourself too thin and have less time in which to sell and produce your product or service.

Using outside services will free you to do what you do best. Another advantage is that the professionals you hire can do a better job at their special tasks than you can.

Phone-Answering Service

If you loathe phone-answering machines, or if you regard them as unprofessional, you can hire an answering service.

Many answering services advertise in local papers and in the Yellow Pages. Before you choose one, call half a dozen or more to ask about rates and get an idea of the quality of the service offered. Also, you may encounter an answering service when calling someone else. If the service impresses you, ask to speak with the manager. In large cities, you may find very reasonably priced answering services that are run by (and primarily for) actors and musicians. Look in the back pages of local actors' and musicians' newspapers.

Overnight Courier

The urgency of business deadlines has created a great demand for the overnight delivery of packages. There are many services to choose from. In addition to private couriers such as Federal Express and Purolator, the U.S. Postal Service offers overnight Express Mail Service. The key considerations are reasonable price and reliability. However, there is no reason to stick with just one service. You can use several or all of them.

Instead of paying for each package as you send it, we suggest you establish credit accounts with the couriers you use on a regular basis. That way, you receive a single, consolidated bill from each courier at the end of the month, which greatly simplifies bookkeeping and payment.

Messenger Service

Businesses in urban locations frequently employ messenger services that can provide same-day delivery of packages within the metropolitan area. Some messenger services offer same-day delivery between major cities, such as New York and Washington, D.C., or Philadelphia.

Call several local services listed in the Yellow Pages, and ask for their rates. Pick the lowest-priced service. If it performs as promised, you will save a lot of money on deliveries.

If it messes up the first job, use the next least expensive service.

Typing Service

At times, you may need an extra hand to do some lengthy or very important typing. A secretarial service or typing service is often the best way to get this sort of thing done on time and in a professional manner. You will find typing services listed in the Yellow Pages and in many trade and business magazines and newspapers. Call several of them, and choose the one whose rates and services best suit your needs.

Here are some questions you may want to ask typing services.

- What kind of equipment do they use? Most use top-of-the-line electronic typewriters or word processors.
- How much do they charge per page? How long will it take them to complete a job of a given length? In an emergency, are they able to respond more quickly?
- Can they handle very large typing jobs?
- Do they pick up and deliver work?
- Do they charge more for word processing than for typing?
- Who provides bond paper for lengthy jobs, you or the service? If the service provides it, what quality is it?

You may at times be as dependent on your typing service as you are on your attorney or your overnight courier, so choose a service carefully, and do not use it a second time unless you are satisfied with its performance.

Printer

Small businesses often use printing services to produce material that is needed in quantities of more than a hundred. To

present a professional image, you will want a printer to do your brochures, price lists, order forms, letterheads, envelopes, business cards, and fliers.

For your next printing job, get bids from three printers. Do not automatically pick the lowest bid. In addition to a fair price, look for reliability, quality of work, availability of paper stock, and fast turnaround time. By getting three bids, you will also know whether one of them is far too high.

Most printing jobs are simple and can be handled by any competent local printshop. Printers that advertise themselves as "quick print," "instant print," and "résumé" shops offer fast turnaround and reasonable prices on small, uncomplicated jobs. For a larger, more complex printing job such as a catalog or a color poster, you may require the services of a larger printshop with special presses and equipment.

Once you have found a competent, reasonably priced printer, it is better to use them for all your printing jobs rather than to spread your work among several shops. You will get better service from a printer if you give him or her a lot of work on a regular basis.

Accountant

An accountant can do three things for you: (1) set up a financial recordkeeping system you can use to keep track of business income and expenses, (2) prepare your income tax returns, and (3) provide tax planning services that will allow you to take advantage of legal ways to pay less tax.

Many self-employed people respond, "I can do my own income tax returns, so why hire an accountant?" There are two reasons: First, your time is valuable, and hiring an accountant to handle income tax returns frees you to concentrate on running your business. Second, and more important, the accountant can do a better job than you can, and

better translates into *tax savings*. Numerous changes are made in the tax laws every year. You can't possibly keep up with them, but your accountant can. His or her tax expertise can save you money and help you avoid the hassles, penalties, and interest charges that result when a return is filed incorrectly.

Many small businesses and self-employed people have their returns prepared by accountants who have full-time jobs with corporations or other organizations but who prepare individual returns in their spare time. Their fees are often lower than those of the large accounting firms. The moonlighter's fee usually ranges from $85 to $250, but you should be prepared to pay more if consulting and tax planning services are included.

Another type of accountant is the full-time accounting firm specializing in tax counseling and return preparation. These firms charge more than moonlighters do, often $350 to $750. A full-time accountant or firm may be better able to keep abreast of the latest tax laws and regulations. In fact, a large or medium-size accounting firm may have several employees who do nothing but read and interpret the latest documents from the Internal Revenue Service. As a result, a big firm can probably find additional legal ways for you to save money on income tax, and those savings could pay for the higher fee many times over.

Lawyer

As an independent businessperson, you will need to consult with a lawyer on a wide range of legal issues, from incorporating your business and understanding zoning laws to handling lawsuits. A good lawyer is indispensable. But where do you find one?

Almost everyone these days either has a lawyer or knows of one. Get the names of several good attorneys from friends and colleagues. Then talk to the lawyers about what they can

do for you and how they charge. Legal fees vary widely from $40 to $250 an hour and up. Generally, the bigger and more prestigious the law firm, the higher the fee.

As a small business, you may find that a smaller law firm is better suited to your needs. There are many free-lance lawyers who can do a good job counseling and representing you.

Look for a small law firm or free-lancer with a good reputation. Personality is also important. You will be confiding in and trusting your lawyer 100 percent, so you should feel as comfortable dealing with him or her as you do talking with a friend.

If the attorney asks for a monthly retainer, go to someone else. As a self-employed individual just starting out in the business world, you will not use enough of the attorney's time to justify a monthly fee. Instead, find an attorney who will work for you by the hour and only when you need legal help. Make sure you can afford the hourly fee; you should reasonably expect to pay $50 to $100 an hour.

Finally, avoid the attorney who seems to keep the meter running all the time. If you get a bill after a ten-minute telephone conversation with your attorney, find a new lawyer immediately. A good professional should be willing to spend a few minutes with a client now and then without one eye on the clock and the other on the invoice ledger.

Sources of Business Information

A self-employed person's education is a continuing process. In addition to gaining experience in running your own business, you will want to broaden and deepen your knowledge of your own field and of the business world in general. Here are a few of the many available ways to do just that.

- *Courses on entrepreneurship.* Some 340 American colleges and universities now offer these courses. Call the schools in your area to find out what is being offered.

- *Seminars.* Business seminars are shorter, and often less expensive, than college courses. They offer a quick way to learn new skills or brush up on old ones. Check with local business associations and the chamber of commerce to learn where and when they are being held.
- *American Society for Training and Development.* By joining ASTD, you will receive *Training* magazine as well as information on courses and seminars being held across the nation. The address is 1630 Duke Street, P.O. Box 1443, Alexandria, VA 22313; (703) 683-8100.
- *Association and trade publications.* These magazines and newspapers carry announcements of various educational opportunities open to businesspeople. Look through the *Business Periodicals Index* at the public library to learn which publications will be helpful to you.

Further Reading

Magazines focusing on small business are available at newsstands or by subscription.

Here are some publications to look for.

Entrepreneur
631 Wilshire Boulevard
Santa Monica, CA 90401

In Business
18 South Seventh Street
Emmaus, PA 18049

Inc.
38 Commercial Wharf
Boston, MA 02110

Journal of Applied Management
1200 Mount Diablo Boulevard
Walnut Creek, CA 94596

Small Business Report
550 Hartnell Street
Monterrey, CA 95940

Venture
521 Fifth Avenue
New York, NY 10175

PART IV

Escape!

7

Countdown to Glory

GETTING READY

Here is the countdown of things you should do to prepare for the day you escape the organization. Naturally, the items and schedule will vary depending on your job, the planned start-up date of your new business venture, and the type of business you are starting. For example, starting a manufacturing company is more complex than starting a free-lance writing business. Use this schedule as a guide only; modify it to suit your particular needs.

Six Months Before You Quit

- Decide exactly what type of business you will start or what profession you will enter.
- Talk to successful people already in the business to get information and advice.
- Begin to acquire whatever specialized knowledge or skills you will need through books, training, college courses, magazines, and so forth.
- Discuss the move with your spouse, family, and close friends.

- Decide on the specific products or services you will offer, how you will produce the products or render the services, whom you will sell to, and why your customers should want to buy from you.
- Start putting money aside.

Three Months Before You Quit

- Choose a name for your company.
- Find an attorney and an accountant.
- File the paper work to set up your business as a legal entity.
- Establish a business checking account.
- Design your letterhead, or hire a graphic designer to do it for you.
- Write your business plan.
- Begin putting out feelers by quietly talking to people in the business to see what the potential market is for your service or product.
- Keep saving money. Set aside savings you can draw on if needed. Avoid long-term investments that would tie up your cash.
- Start looking at office space, or figure out how you will set up an office at home.
- Write ads, brochures, sales letters, flip chart presentations, and other advertising and promotional materials.
- Manufacturers: Begin to manufacture prototypes, and set up your manufacturing operation.
- Distributors: Seek out suppliers you can buy from at reasonable prices. Make your initial contacts with these suppliers.

One Month Before You Quit

- Print business cards and letterheads.
- Rent office space or set up home office.

- Start buying necessary office equipment such as a typewriter, desk, chair, bookcases.
- Get a telephone-answering machine, or hire an answering service.
- Hand in your letter of resignation.
- Begin actively soliciting business, making contacts, and letting people know about your company.
- Print brochures and sales letters.
- Create final versions of slides, flip charts, and other presentation aids.
- Start a file of prospective clients.
- Begin to arrange appointments and to call on clients.
- Manufacturers: Buy raw materials.
- Distributors: Establish a line of credit with suppliers.
- Establish a line of credit with printers, magazines (for space advertising), office supply dealers, and other vendors.
- Have your accountant set up a bookkeeping system and show you how to use it.

Two Weeks Before You Quit

- Tell co-workers what you are doing, and give them your business card.
- Assemble samples of your work—reports, photos, memos, products—to show potential customers.
- Send out direct mail and place advertisements.
- Increase selling activities; try to close sales if possible.
- Tie up any loose ends at the organization. Transfer projects to others who will be responsible for them.
- Consult with your accountant to make sure you are keeping proper records.
- Consult with your lawyer to make sure all necessary licenses, permits, and applications have been obtained.
- Move into your new office.
- Buy any equipment and supplies that you still need.

- Notify all outside vendors of your move; send them your card.
- Check with the personnel department about termination of benefits and any money owed to you by the company.

One Week Before You Quit

- Write a status report on all your organization projects, indicating current status and people responsible.
- Take your property home, and clean out your desk.
- Say good-bye to colleagues and associates.
- Take your boss and immediate co-workers out for a farewell lunch.

Your Last Day

- Stay for the entire day. Attend the farewell party.
- Take one last look around the place.
- Walk out the door, and don't look back. You are free now. You are on your own.

RESIGNING

Okay, you are ready to resign. This section should answer all those questions in your mind.

When Should I Resign?

Once you announce your resignation, there is no turning back. So don't resign until you are ready—emotionally and financially. Here are some of the things that may be worrying you.

- *I haven't saved enough money!* If you are constantly worrying about money, you have not yet reached your *comfort level*, the point at which you have enough money in the bank. Build your savings until you feel financially secure before you hand in your resignation.

- *I'm not sure this is really what I want to do.* The time to decide on your new career is before you resign, not after. Don't quit until you have defined what your new venture will be.
- *I haven't prepared myself enough for this new venture.* You should do most of the planning for your new business while you have your old job. The business should basically be set up and ready to run the day you leave.
- *I am scared!* Anxiety and nervousness go with the territory. You will be quitting a secure position for the uncertainties of free-lance life. But if you are frightened to the point where you feel frozen and are unable to function, you are not ready to take the plunge.
- *I feel pressed for time.* Maybe you feel pressured because you still have many details to take care of before you are on your own. Go back over Part III of this book and complete any tasks you may have neglected. Resigning from a job to start a business is a major change in your life. Don't make it until you are ready.

We are sure there are more questions lurking there in the back of your mind and gnawing at your resolve. Let's root them out and put them to rest, too.

Should I Wait Around to Collect My Next Bonus?

No, not if you have reached your savings goal. "Why not?" you ask. "I could stick it out a little while longer and collect some extra cash." But there will *always* be something coming up—a bonus, a raise, a new project, a vacation, a business trip to a foreign country, a promotion. If you wait for the bonus, why not wait for the raise so that you can tell people you were making an annual salary of Y instead of X? If you wait to qualify for an extra week's vacation, why not wait until your employment anniversary so that your résumé shows five years of service instead of only four?

There is always something to wait for. A person who waits will probably keep on waiting and never leave. To escape the

organization, you must break corporate bonds. And that means giving up those future bonuses, raises, and perks. So when you are ready to resign, do it. Don't wait, no matter what the company promises for the future.

How Much Notice Should I Give?

If you are a professional, you will give a month's notice. For support staff and blue-collar workers, two weeks is customary, Actually, these are just suggested time periods. Unless you are bound by an employment contract, giving *any* advanced notice is simply a courtesy that you extend to your employer.

It is a vital courtesy, however, if you want to leave on good terms. In general, the higher up on the ladder you are, the more notice you should give.

What If the Boss Asks Me to Stay Longer?

Employers frequently pressure employees to stay on until they can train or hire a replacement. Sometimes, this comes as a request, other times, it is a subtle threat. Someone may hint that you won't receive a good recommendation unless you stick it out a little longer.

Don't give in to requests or threats. It is simply a way of preventing you from making a clean break with the corporation. Stand by your schedule and resignation date. If the company insists that it needs your services desperately, you can offer to work for it on a part-time basis as a consultant— at double or triple your old rate of pay. Such an arrangement is not unusual; employees who resign often find that their former employer becomes their first client.

Should I Resign in Person or by Letter?

It depends on your relationship with your boss. If you do not get along, or if you anticipate a negative reaction, do it by

letter. A letter shows you mean business and makes it harder for the boss to talk you out of your resignation. On the other hand, if the boss is a friend, someone you respect, like, and admire, and if the two of you are close, you will probably want to tell him or her in person. Make sure to do it in private, at a time when you can chat in a free and relaxed manner. Also, bring a letter along with your new business card enclosed, and hand it over after you have had your discussion.

Here is a good letter of resignation.

Mr. Ron Taylor
Vice President, Production
Americom Communications
Anytown, U.S.

Dear Ron:

On June 15, I will be resigning from my position as plant manager, Avionics Division. I have enjoyed working under you during my years with Americom. But as you know, I have always talked about setting up my own electronics testing firm some day. Well, June 15 will be that day!

I appreciate all the help and guidance you have given me, and I will miss working with you and the crew in Avionics. If I can ever help you in any way, give me a call.

Sincerely,

Bob Blank
Plant Manager

This letter contains the essential elements.

1. The tone is polite and friendly, not superior or haughty.
2. It gives the important news right away (that the manager is leaving on June 15).
3. The writer shows his appreciation for his boss and the company and what they have done for him.
4. The writer provides an explanation for his resignation that is truthful without being smug or offensive.
5. The writer does *not* make the mistake of venting anger, taking a parting shot, or getting a long-standing complaint off his chest. A resignation letter is *not* a means of getting even. It is a way of ending a relationship without hard feelings.

Your boss should be the first to get the news of your resignation, and the letter should be addressed to him or her. Later on, you can send copies to the boss's boss, your departmental supervisor, and the personnel department, but make sure your boss has received *and read* your letter before these copies are distributed. Regardless of your relationship, your boss has the right to hear it from you first. He or she should not find out from gossip at the water cooler.

LEAVING ON FRIENDLY TERMS

Even if you have spent the past five years in abject misery, hating your job, your co-workers, your boss, and the company's vendors, you cannot afford to leave the organization on anything but the best-possible terms. The vendor who was rude to you last week may, after all, be the only person in town who can provide exactly the right machine parts for your new company. And the manager who walked all over you last year could someday become one of your best customers.

What we are saying is that no matter how angry you are, there is simply no percentage in popping off at people during your last days on the job. Control your resentment, modulate your feelings, and leave the organization without rancor.

Here are some do's and don'ts to remember during your last weeks on the job.

Do's

Do cooperate with the people who will carry on your function until a replacement can be found. Answer their questions, and provide the materials they need.

Do offer your assistance even if it is not asked for. One successful entrepreneur took it upon himself to write up a job description for his replacement, saving his boss the trouble of doing it. This simple courtesy was much appreciated; to this day, the entrepreneur and his former boss keep in touch.

Do cooperate with your replacement. Offer a helping hand. Show the newcomer your files and your current projects, and introduce him or her to the people you work with on a daily basis. Your successor might someday return the favor by becoming a client.

Do tie up loose ends. Don't drop the ball on important projects simply because they soon won't be your problem anymore. Finish as many projects as possible. Bring the others to a stage where someone else can take over.

Do write a job manual and status report for your successor. A job manual is an informal memo that contains the tips, techniques, resources, methods, and other specialized knowledge about doing the job that you have picked up over the years. A status report is a list of all current projects and the status of each. This report ensures that important projects are not neglected because of a lack of awareness on the part of your successor.

Do offer to be available to answer brief questions or give quick advice after you leave your job. Make it clear, however, that you will charge a consulting fee for extensive, time-consuming advice.

Do keep in touch with friends within the company. You will enjoy maintaining this bond. And again, keeping your name in front of people as a potential source of services can never hurt.

Don'ts

Don't boast about your new venture. It will only annoy others.

Don't let things slide. You still have responsibilities to the employer paying your salary. Finish as much of your work as possible. If you leave chaos behind you when you depart, people will remember your negligence and forget the years of good work you did for the corporation.

Don't neglect nonmanagement employees during your last days on the job. Remember that today's office boy or receptionist could become tomorrow's top manager and perhaps an important client.

FINANCIAL MATTERS

Escaping the organization is not without its emotional and monetary costs. For when you leave the corporation, you may give up many financial benefits, such as:

- Steady paycheck
- Bonuses
- Free health insurance
- Free life insurance
- Free dental insurance
- Pension
- Savings plan
- Expense account

Many of these benefits will end the minute you leave the corporation. And some of these perks, especially insurance, you cannot afford to be without. Therefore, *now* is the time to replace the insurance and financial benefits you will lose.

Health, Disability, and Life Insurance

The most important extra the corporation gives you is free health insurance. Your coverage under the company's group health plan will end the day you quit or shortly thereafter (check your benefits package for the exact date). Therefore, you should start shopping for a new health plan right now. Arrange to have the new health insurance go into effect on the day your old coverage runs out. You should *never* be without health insurance, not even for *one day.*

The cost of health care is so high that a single illness or accident could cost tens of thousands of dollars. A long-term illness or serious accident could quickly drain your life savings and put you into bankruptcy if you are not covered by health insurance. And you *cannot* buy insurance to pay bills *after* the accident happens or the disease is diagnosed. To protect yourself and your family against financial disaster, call your insurance agent *before you resign,* and ask about a health plan that suits your needs. If your company's health plan allows you to convert from group to individual coverage, let your agent know.

The cost of such a policy—anywhere from $500 to $1,500 a year or more, depending on the coverage provided—may come as a shock to you, especially because your insurance has been free until now. But don't make the mistake of trying to save money by not buying health insurance. Every day you walk around without coverage is a day you are inviting financial disaster to strike.

As a self-employed person, you may be forced to buy an individual policy. This costs much more than a group policy, which covers a large number of individuals who work in the same organization. One way to save money on insurance is to

find a group offering low-cost insurance, join it, and sign up for the insurance. Many professional societies, social groups, and trade associations (e.g., American Institute of Chemical Engineers, B'nai B'rith) offer group insurance to their members. The money you save on insurance premiums pays the membership cost many times over.

What would you do if you became ill or disabled and were unable to work? Long-term disability insurance pays you money each month if such a problem ever occurs. The more money the insurance pays per month, the higher the premium will be. Try to get enough disability insurance to cover all your expenses (mortgage, utility bills, food, clothing) in case you become totally disabled.

Insurance companies sometimes make it difficult for self-employed people, especially those just starting out, to get a lot of disability insurance. The reason is that you, as a self-employed individual, do not have an established income. Therefore, you cannot prove that if you are disabled, you will lose X dollars a week in income you would have earned. If you cannot get as much disability as you want, take the maximum the insurance company will give you. Upgrade your coverage later on when you get established in your business.

Depending on the terms of your policy, it can take thirty, sixty, or ninety days before the insurance company is required to begin paying after you become disabled. By choosing the ninety-day option, you can significantly reduce your premium.

If you have dependents, life insurance can provide for them if you die. Ask your insurance agent about the many life insurance options available. Some types, such as universal life, are also investments that grow in cash value as years go by. Others have no investment value but do have far lower annual premiums. Some life insurance policies have *vanishing premiums,* meaning that after a number of years, you have bought the policy and do not have to pay anymore. Some policies require a payment every year.

Retirement Plans

As a self-employed worker, you do not have a company investing in a pension, savings plan, or other retirement account for you. Therefore, you will have to create your own retirement fund. The two investment vehicles most commonly used for this are the individual retirement account (IRA) and the Keogh.

The current law allows any individual worker, self-employed or not, to put up to $2,000 each year in an IRA. A couple can invest up to $4,000 when both are working, $2,250 when only one spouse is working.

The IRA is a *tax-deferred* investment, not tax-free. You *will* have to pay tax on the money in your IRA, and those taxes become payable and due when you retire and draw the money out of the account, which can be anywhere from age 59 1/2 to age 70 1/2.

(NOTE: Since the tax bill of 1986 was passed as this book went to press, we suggest you consult with your accountant concerning any restrictions on IRAs and Keoghs.)

A Keogh is similar to an IRA, but it allows you to set aside even more money in a tax-deferred account. And unlike IRAs, which are available to everyone, only self-employed people are eligible for Keoghs. According to *J. K. Lasser's Guide to Tax-Deferred Investments* (New York: Simon & Schuster, 1985), you can put up to 20 percent of your net income *or* $30,000, whichever is smaller, into a Keogh for your retirement.

By using both an IRA and a Keogh, you can significantly lower your tax payments for the year. Most financial experts agree that IRAs and Keoghs are among the best investments that self-employed people can make.

Benefit Transfers and Entitlements

A few employers will extend their benefits beyond the resignation date, either as a gift to the departing employee or in

return for a monthly fee. This extension gives you a much-welcome breather in the hectic period of transition from corporate life to career independence. Continuing your benefits for another month or two keeps you covered while you shop for the insurance plans and retirement accounts that are right for you.

Check to see if your company offers an extension of benefits. If it does so at a reasonable cost, take advantage of it until you are settled in your new routine. Meanwhile, shop around for replacements.

Don't cut yourself off from your company's treasure chest just yet. You may find that you are entitled to all sorts of financial benefits, including:

- Back pay for vacations not taken
- Back pay for sick days not taken
- Back pay for overtime worked
- Extra severance pay
- Use of your old office for a period of time
- Use of certain company perks, such as your discount card for car rentals or air travel, for a period of time
- Continuation of savings programs such as credit unions and retirement accounts
- Money from the pension fund, credit union, stockholdings, or other accounts

Be sure to ask about any benefits that may be due to you. If you don't investigate, you may lose out on a lot of money and other extras. Speak up! No one else is going to do it for you.

8

Those Who Lived to Tell the Tale

PROFILES IN SELF-EMPLOYMENT SUCCESS

Up until now, we have established what it takes to cross the bridge from corporate employment to self-employment. But how do people really cope with the many seemingly overwhelming tasks involved with beginning a business? In this chapter, we meet five people, including one couple, who left the organization to make it on their own and who have succeeded.

Tom and Pat Sprecher

Tom and Pat Sprecher run Corporate Book Resources, a mail order book house in Rutherford, New Jersey. At first, Pat, who was working for a company that sold cruises, ran the business part-time in the evenings. As it grew, Tom, an executive recruiter, quit his job to pitch in. Six months later, Pat also left her job to devote herself to the business full-time.

Did Pat and Tom have any qualms about quitting steady jobs for what was admittedly a calculated risk? Surprisingly, no. Their children were grown and gone. They had previous

experience with supporting themselves through real estate investments. Their living expenses were low. And both had dreamed for many years of starting their own business.

"I had always wanted to work for myself," says Tom. "I never had a desire to work for an enormous company for thirty or forty years and climb a predetermined career ladder."

The major obstacle that had held them back from making a move earlier was the lack of money. Fortunately, this new book-ordering business required a minimal capital investment. Security was never a major concern. Both Pat and Tom had worked in a variety of fields—Tom as a psychologist, writer, real estate broker, and executive recruiter; Pat as a secretary, real estate broker, and travel agent.

Although they both are putting in longer hours now than they did working for others, they feel the effort is worth it. Tom says, "At this point, it is more important to me to enjoy what I am doing. Our satisfaction comes from working with books, something we both love. And if I work sixty hours a week instead of forty, the difference shows up in the business."

Another reason they had always wanted to start their own business was to have control over what they were doing. Now, as their own bosses with one part-time employee, the Sprechers handle problems their own way. "There is no one to account to, and no political games to play," emphasizes Tom. "The down side is that you worry more. We have had our ups and downs, but we try to help each other keep things in perspective."

The fact that Tom was fifty-seven and Pat was fifty-three when they started the business full-time in late 1984 made them determined to succeed. Says Pat, "Once we started, we knew we had to stick it out since it would be very difficult for Tom to find another job if it failed."

In the past two years, the business has grown steadily to the point where Tom and Pat have rented outside office

space and moved to a new apartment. But they still worry about the business, and a slow week can cause some sleepless nights. "We're not yet making as much money as we did working for others, but the potential is there," says Pat. "I am glad we started off on a part-time basis because there are more details involved in running a business than we had realized."

In fact, it is a constant learning experience of finding ways to save money and to do things more efficiently. For example, after a year of typing invoices one at a time, the couple invested in a personal computer that has cut down substantially on the billing work.

Their advice to those aspiring to become self-employed is: Go into a business you know or can learn by working for someone else first. Then, know what you are up against in terms of competition. "Focus on a target market, and be willing to refine your ideas and operation as you go along," Pat offers. "But don't wait until everything is perfect, or you will never do it."

Eileen Kelly

After her divorce ten years ago, Eileen Kelly went back to work as an administrative assistant. Although she was frustrated because her boss resisted her attempts to take on additional responsibilities, it was not until she was fired that she found the courage to go into business for herself. Now Eileen runs a "quasi-franchise" operation, working as a full-time sales consultant for Carlisle Collection Limited, an importer of high-quality executive clothes for women.

Because Eileen had started selling clothes for the company on a part-time basis while still working as an administrative assistant, she had a pretty good idea of what to expect. Still, that first week without a regular paycheck was scary.

"I didn't have much self-confidence," Eileen confesses. "I

was frightened because I had never run my own business with the goal of having it completely support me." She had to lay out money for supplies, buy her own medical and life insurance, and set up the business in her home. There, she sells the company's clothes; writes and designs her own sales materials; handles marketing, merchandising, and deliveries; and collects the bills from which she deducts her sales commission. For a fee, the Carlisle Collection, which is based in New York City, supplies each season's clothing collection, sponsors quarterly sales training sessions, mails a weekly newsletter with sales tips, and provides some supplies.

"It was hard at first," says Eileen. "Sales is a business that builds slowly. And running your own business, you have a tendency to be too hard on yourself."

One of her biggest challenges has been convincing people she is a professional. "Some people think because I work at home, my business isn't really serious," Eileen says. "Whether it's potential clients or friends, that bothers me." But that attitude has changed as her sales and her self-confidence have grown. "When I saw other consultants making monumental sales, I just decided that if they could do it, so could I. And I also learned to tune out negative attitudes from other people. You can't let them influence you."

Would Eileen ever go back to working in a regular job? Not if she can help it. Despite the downs of working for herself, Eileen has gotten quite attached to the ups. "I like being in charge. And I like the fact that I am competing with myself, not with others. I don't have to consult with other people before I do something. Companies have a framework you have to work within that can be stifling. Now I have the chance to be more innovative and creative."

Even the snowstorm during her last showing week that caused half her appointments not to show up did not make her throw in the towel. "Many times, I have thought of dumping the whole thing. Maybe it is Murphy's law, but everything bad seems to happen at once," says Eileen. "What

keeps me going is my enthusiasm for the work and my determination to prove I can make this business go."

Steve Brown

After graduating from the School of Visual Arts in New York City in 1970, Stephen Brown worked as an art director for a magazine, an advertising agency, and at an art gallery. Then he had a fight with a manager on the staff and found himself unemployed. Ever since, he has been working as a free-lance graphic artist, happily running his own business.

"I would never, never go back to a 'regular' job," says Steve. "It's fantastic to be your own boss. As someone who likes to live it up at night, I can sleep late and work the hours I choose." The material rewards aren't so bad, either. He is about to fulfill a lifelong dream by buying twenty-six acres in Vermont and building a log cabin for weekend getaways.

The road to financial independence has been rocky, though. It began ten years ago, when Steve worked as a free-lancer for two friends who had set up their own design studio.

"Their business was up and down," says Steve. So when one of the partners walked out, Steve walked out, too, and set up shop in a studio on Forty-second Street in New York City. "That was my lowest point," recalls Steve. "I sat there day after day, waiting for the phone to ring, hoping something would break. I would drink a half-pint of Bacardi rum and stare out the window."

Finally, Steve got his big break. He won the advertising account of a Japanese manufacturer. Along with a partner who acted as account executive, Steve went into running his own business full-time. Although both his partner and the account have since departed, he is, as he puts it, "one thousand percent better off than in my Bacardi rum days."

One reason is that he has learned how to network and sell himself. "Creative people seem to dislike selling themselves,"

he observes. "But I attend seminars on the subject because I know you have to sell to be successful." As for networking, one bar contact has supplied Steve with clients for one and a half years.

A growth in self-esteem has helped, too. "I used to have a tremendous lack of self-confidence," says Steve. "I figured my lot in life would be to just get by as a jack-of-all-trades free-lancer." That attitude has changed as clients express their satisfaction with Steve's work. "Now I know I'm a good designer, but my real strength lies in being a good listener and giving good service. And when customers are happy with your work, they will keep coming back."

Like many self-employed people, Steve found that the hardest part of this venture was adjusting to an erratic cash flow. "It can take months to get paid after completing a job," he points out. "So you can be doing very well but have a lot of money outstanding." For that reason, Steve keeps his expenses low and maintains at least a $4,000 cushion of savings in the bank.

Another persistent danger is that a major client can pull out his or her business at any time. "Unfortunately, most free-lancers I know, including myself, always seem to have one or two clients who provide them with the bulk of their income," Steve says. "And there is a tendency to get complacent about going after new business when you are busy."

Through the years, he has come around to thinking in terms of his business as a long-term commitment. And there are just too many things he likes about being his own boss to contemplate getting a traditional job again.

Roger Parker

At forty-three, Roger Parker feels as if he is starting his life over. He has been running his own business for ten years, but now he has the self-confidence and self-knowledge to feel good about not being a part of the corporate world.

That realization was recently reinforced when he spent three months working in a company office. "Somehow I had gotten the attitude that because I did not work at a large, prestigious company, I wasn't as good or 'real' as other people," he says. "Once I tried working for a company again, I found out it's okay to have a small office. Now I have come back with a certain dignity I didn't have before."

Roger started his own business when he was fired from his job as advertising manager for a retail chain because of a personality conflict with the owner. "Since then, I've decided I trust my own inadequacies more than I trust others and their inadequacies," says Roger. "When you fail on your own, you can easily recognize the cause and correct it. When you succeed, you get to take the credit."

As the owner of, first, the Roger C. Parker Advertising Center and, now, The Write Word, he provides copywriting and consulting services in advertising and marketing. He disbanded the Advertising Center when it grew to more than six employees. "The size took the fun out of it," he explains. "I like being a one-person operation."

From the beginning, Roger's businesses have been financially successful. Although he made more mistakes than he will ever let anyone know, Roger rebounded from them quickly. "The first year was utopia," he says. "I refuse to believe that you cannot make money right away. If you're competent and enthusiastic, you will."

In terms of economic impact, he finds the things that are the easiest for him to do bring him the most money and the greatest success. The things he struggles with are the least profitable. As his own attitudes change, his business changes, so that he is continually redefining what he does and how he does it.

For a while, Roger handled mostly "long-distance" copywriting, serving clients by mail and phone. Now, he prefers more face-to-face contact. "I think my earlier approach was a reflection of wanting to hide from people," he says. "Now, I have more self-confidence."

He divides his time between two offices, one at home, one rented. He finds he gets sidetracked and loses his motivation unless he gets out of the house.

As the father of three boys, Roger readily acknowledges his goal is to make a lot of money. But he loves the freedom of being able to take off early to spend time with his sons. "I don't mind being a workaholic," he states, "but I want to do it on my own terms." So, Roger regularly works Sunday evenings from 7:00 P.M. to 2:00 A.M. but often takes Monday mornings off.

Roger believes that times have changed since his father's day. "His generation felt that the company would always be there and always take care of them. It just isn't so today. Look at the oil and steel industries. I'd rather be unemployed through my own fault than someone else's."

The best advice Roger Parker can offer to someone who wants to start a business is to use time as wisely as possible. He groans, "I would spend hours writing an article for a magazine that no potential clients would read." Now he knows better and spends the bulk of his time on profitable activities.

Roger is the first to admit that it has taken him a long time to realize his strengths and find his niche. And he still is not sure what the future holds for his business. But whatever he decides, he now knows that the skills that helped him succeed in the past will work in the future, too. "It took me a long time to learn a hard lesson: The things you think you are instinctively good at, the world will think you are good at, too."

All these individuals have made it on their own, almost to their own surprise. It is interesting to note that in some of the cases, the decision to leave the corporation was not solely their own. Certainly, the individualistic qualities that cause friction or discontent in the corporate office are also the qualities that will help a person to succeed when he or she chooses career independence. We deliberately chose people

who are not millionaire entrepreneurs because they represent the majority of the self-employed. They are the ones who lead financially secure lives within their own businesses, enjoying all the benefits of autonomy other than million-dollar net worths.

who are about?tion[?e] ?erogeneous besides. Thus who
?sp??d the ??mber of these ?e explained. ?ou? ?e the ??a
who had ???entially ???? ?roswho in ?ell the? business
?onsider their interest, or among ?a other, ?hat the public
?really ???t? based.

PART
V

Life After Escape

9

Coping in the Self-Employed World

DEALING WITH THE SHOCK OF INDEPENDENCE

Escaping the organization is a jolt to your system. Suddenly, you are thrust into a new work universe with a different set of rules. Gone are the daily commutes, the bull sessions, the meetings, the memos, the ringing phones, the efficient secretaries, the modular offices, the big budgets, and the wealth of corporate resources. Now, you are on your own.

You may feel ill at ease during this initial period. It's natural to be uncomfortable in new and strange situations, and it may take several months for you to feel truly relaxed and at home in your new role.

We have identified some of the causes of shock, and we have a few suggestions for getting rid of those butterflies in your stomach.

The "It's Too Quiet" Syndrome

The Symptoms Your tiny office is quiet, and you cannot stand it. The solitude and peacefulness are driving you crazy. Where are all the busy people? Why are there no interruptions?

153

The Cure Create activities for yourself, especially activities involving people. Spend half a day on the telephone catching up with old colleagues, friends, and acquaintances. Renew social contacts over drinks and lunch or dinner. Arrange meetings with potential clients or customers. Go to some meetings or parties, and do some networking to broaden your base of contacts. Getting out into the world is the best cure for this syndrome.

The Money Drain Syndrome

The Symptoms Your business has not generated much income yet, but you still have to pay your bills. Your bank account is diminishing alarmingly; and frankly, that makes you nervous. You ask yourself, "Was I wrong to give up that weekly paycheck? Where is the money when I need it?"

The Cure Add up your assets: checking account, savings, IRA, stocks, bonds, real estate, insurance, collectibles. You will see that you really have more money than you thought. Cut back on unnecessary expenses and luxury items, and stop worrying.

The "I Don't Have a Job" Syndrome

The Symptoms You know you are working, but you feel unemployed. Real workers, you think, commute and have modular offices and administrative assistants.

The Cure Behave like a working person, not a jobless man or woman. Wear businesslike clothes every day. You won't feel like a bum if you look like a professional. Keep up your subscription to the *Wall Street Journal,* and retain some of the corporate rituals that made you feel a part of the work world.

The Twilight Zone Syndrome

The Symptoms You have escaped the organization, but your new life seems unreal to you. You know you have become a company, but you do not feel like a company. Real companies, you think, are traded on the New York Stock Exchange and have offices in Tokyo, Paris, Hong Kong, and London. Your office is in the basement, and the only thing you trade is baseball cards.

The Cure Do things that will make your company seem more real, both to outsiders and to yourself. Run some advertisements. Print a brochure describing your company, and distribute it to potential clients. Get your company listed in industry directories, right next to the big guns. At the next special event or Christmas party of your industry trade association, donate a gift for a door prize or drawing *in the name of your company.* That is one way to let people know you are real.

The Pure Panic Syndrome

The Symptoms You have already been in the business for three whole weeks, and you have not made a million dollars yet. You have not been invited to the White House to advise the president on business matters. You haven't been on the cover of *Time* magazine yet.

The Cure Relax. No one said starting and running a business would provide instant gratification. The truth is, building a successful business takes patience, time, and hard work.

Assess your achievements on a monthly, rather than daily, basis. Do not fly into a panic just because it is Monday and the phone is not ringing off the hook. As we have already said, there may be days, even weeks, when business is quiet. You have to take it all in stride.

Another way to get rid of pure panic is to close a sale, even

if you have to lower your profit margin to do so. Just having the business locked up will give you a sense of accomplishment and relieve your frenzy. Free-lance writer Milt Pierce says, "It is better to work for a little money than not work at all."

The "I Can't Take Rejection" Syndrome

The Symptoms You lose your first sale, and you are crushed. You realize that people can live without your service or product, and that scares you. You realize that other people—prospects, customers, clients, buyers—still have some control over your life, and that depresses you. You take the rejection personally, and that makes you feel terrible. You think you will never regain the opportunity you just lost, and that scares you, too.

The Cure Believe it or not, the more you get rejected, the more likely you are to succeed! If you are getting rejections, that means you are out there selling. People who never fail are people who never try, and those are the people who never succeed.

The cure in this case is to get back out there and sell even harder. The more you sell, the greater your chances of success. Let's say you have the potential to turn 1 percent of your prospects into paying customers. If you approach only 1 person, the odds are 100 to 1 against success. But if you get out and sell to 500 people, a 1 percent closing rate will bring you five sales! Only by playing the percentages (and working on your sales ability to increase the closing ratio) can you bring in business, orders, and money.

Also realize that buyers are *not* out to get you. They have to make a buying decision that is right for them or for the company they represent. For some, your product or service is right; for others, it is not. Buyers are just trying to make the best decision, so don't take their rejections personally.

COPING WITH ISOLATION

If you work alone, you may have some trouble getting used to solitude. Isolation can be oppressive if you do not learn how to cope with it. Says one consultant, "The worst thing I have to face is loneliness. I always used to have colleagues to bounce ideas off of. Now I have to do everything by myself."

Not necessarily. Try to build up a network of contacts who will give you feedback on your ideas and who understand the problems of working alone. Get in a people-meeting frame of mind. Start conversations with people in line at supermarkets or photocopy shops or office supply stores. Call to renew your acquaintance with people you have met at trade shows, conventions, and seminars. If you meet someone in the laundry room or in the elevator, invite him or her in for a cup of tea or coffee. You are not the only one who works alone. There are plenty of other people like you, and some of them may live in your building or down the block. Go out to lunch. You will see others who are not dressed for corporate life. Obviously, they are fellow escapees from the nine-to-five world. There are a lot of free-lancers out there. All you have to do is find them.

For some people who work alone, boredom can be worse than solitude. If work comes in regularly, you might not have this problem. But there will be days when time hangs heavy. Take a morning or afternoon off on impulse, but not more than once a week. Go to a movie or have a long lunch or read a novel.

Another suggestion: Schedule at least one meeting a week outside your office, even if it is not absolutely necessary. Interacting with people is refreshing, and the mind needs refreshment.

Vary your work. Take on a project that challenges you, preferably a job that is outside your area of expertise.

When things are slow, cut back your hours. Work from 9:00 A.M. to 4:30 P.M. instead of from 8:00 A.M. to 6:00 P.M. When you are not working, relax.

People need certain rituals to get them through the week. Now that you are no longer at a company, you may be astounded at the amount of time available to you. No one is telling you when to start work or when to stop. You can eat when you want; you can turn on the T.V. You can do what you like *when* you like. But despite the freedom, you may feel a need for ritual. Maybe you could get together with a neighbor or friend for late afternoon coffee or tea, or maybe listen to the news at midday. Rituals can break up the day and also add a sense of structure to it.

Can you use solitude to your advantage? Because you are alone, you can work in a way that is pleasing to you. Maybe you want to listen to music while you write letters. Or perhaps you choose to work in your underwear. Who's to stop you?

Don Burr of People Express values his solitude. He develops his plans and strategies away from the office during his daily run. Good ideas can crop up at any time. You may decide to visit a museum. As you wander through the galleries, an idea may strike. Don't think that all of your ideas will come to you when you try to get them during so-called business hours.

Loneliness is the dark side of privacy. But you can now regulate the flow of people through your life. You may not have instant access to a friend, but you always have access to people who can chat for a moment or two. There will be times when you yearn for more structure. There will be times when you will think savage thoughts about people who promise to call you back but never do. There will be times when you will not get the check and won't be able to express your disappointment to anyone but your cat. (Cats and dogs, by the way, are wonderful antidotes for work-at-home loneliness.)

Pretty soon, as you get busier, the days will go by more quickly, and you will think of a hundred things you can do to

build your business. You will use time better, and you will learn how to integrate solitude with companionship. You will also learn to recognize the times when you need to play hooky for half a day.

The way in which you set up your day can help enhance the variety of your self-employed life. So, having admitted that isolation is a perennial problem, let's now turn our attention to the techniques for managing your time for maximum results.

TIME MANAGEMENT

Getting Used to Your Own Hours

After you leave the organization, you will find that unstructured time is both a delight and a curse. It's a delight in that the company no longer controls your life; it cannot dictate when you wake up, eat lunch, have meetings, take vacations, and leave the office. And you no longer have to make your natural rhythms conform to the corporation's schedule. You can work evenings, if you wish, or even from noon to eight, if that suits you. You can eat lunch at three o'clock.

But you will have to face the fact that, in the real world, most of the work gets done between nine and five, and therein lies a potential problem. In order to keep in touch with your clients and customers, you may have to get on that telephone early in the morning, like it or not. And if the business lunch is your primary means of keeping in touch, you are going to have to get dressed and go out at a time that suits your client—again, like it or not. In short, you will have to confront two common myths about the unstructured time of the self-employed.

The first myth is this: *You work when you want to work.* As we just pointed out, the reality is that you will have to work

when your clients work. You may not have to adhere to a rigid nine-to-five schedule, but you will have to haul yourself out of bed at a reasonable hour.

The second myth is this: *Self-employed people can do exactly the amount of work they want to do.* Again, not always true. As a free-lancer, you are very likely to face the well-known feast-or-famine cycle. In February, you may find yourself working extra long and extra hard to complete an exceptionally large number of jobs. A month later, you may be staring at the walls and wondering why the phone has not rung.

Recognize peaks and lulls as normal. Plan for the peak periods by doing errands, writing letters, and preparing materials during the lulls.

In addition to those two myths, however, there are some delightful realities about self-employment. One of them is that you can take immediate action without being slowed down by the machinery of a large organization.

Whereas NBC might take six months to develop a new logo, you can create one in an afternoon. You need not spend tons of bureaucratic time deciding on a letterhead, business cards, what kind of typewriter to buy, or how to requisition manila folders. You can simply *decide* and then *do.* The same thing is true for hiring and firing employees; you have a free hand to hire and fire quickly.

When a prospective client calls you and asks for some literature about your company, you can promise to put it in the mail immediately because you know that it can and will be done. You are also able to move appointments around with greater ease because you have created your own schedule, know the relative worth of each appointment, and need not check with the boss before reaching for your coat.

Managing Your Time Efficiently

The person who first said that time is money must have been self-employed. Although time management is important for

managers both inside and outside a large organization, self-employed people know that using time well can make the difference between survival and starvation.

Here is a list of time-management tips that are of special importance for the self-employed. They can save you time—time that you can use to bring in the extra client, the extra sale, the contract that could keep you afloat.

Set priorities. Make a list of things you must do. Then number each item on the list. Tasks of greatest importance will be numbered 1; those of secondary importance will be 2; the least important will be numbered 3. Then set out to accomplish each task in 1-2-3 order.

Assess your actions regularly. Several times each day, stop working and ask yourself: Is what I'm doing right now the most important thing I could be doing? If the answer is no, move on to a more vital task.

Avoid doing the easy tasks first Don't fall into the bad habit of performing a number-3-priority task simply because it is easy and can be accomplished quickly. Put it off until the big jobs are done.

Arrange your work schedule to fit your life. If you are a morning person, do your most important tasks before noon. If all of your phone calls seem to come in between three and five o'clock, don't schedule number-1-priority tasks for that time.

Use small blocks of time wisely. You will be amazed how many business letters you can write while waiting for a client to return your telephone call. In just five minutes, while you are waiting for a messenger, you could go through your mail, write several checks, and jot down your ideas for a new project.

Make time for nonwork necessities. Build into your workday or your after-work hours a time to exercise, do business and personal errands, and talk to your friends and family.

Organize your work space efficiently. If you have to spend several minutes digging through your supply closet every

time you need a stamp or an envelope, you are not using your time effectively. Organize your storage space so that you can find things immediately, and *keep it organized.*

Delegate tasks when possible. Must you type every letter and answer every telephone call yourself? Or would it be better to hire a secretary or assistant to relieve you of those chores and thus allow you to spend your time on tasks that will actually produce a profit? If you absolutely refuse to delegate authority, your business is doomed to be forever small.

Further Reading

The following books will give you more information on time management:

Broadwell, Martin M. *The New Supervisor.* New York: Scribner's, 1984.

Drucker, Peter F. *The Efficient Executive.* New York: Harper & Row, 1966.

Ferner, Jack D. *Successful Time Management.* New York: John Wiley & Sons, 1980.

Januz, Lauren R. and Susan K. Jones. *Time Management for Executives.* New York: Scribner's, 1982.

Winston, Stephanie. *The Organized Executive.* New York: Warner Books, 1978.

MAKING TIME FOR YOURSELF

As you start out on your adventure in career independence, you may find yourself thinking about work all the time. You are quite likely to be so caught up in the excitement of your new enterprise that you work longer hours than you really have to. This is perfectly natural, but you must recognize that you need some time away from the job. Only by relaxing now and then and getting your mind off your work can you avoid burning out.

For example, take Mary Walter, owner and founder of two full-service retail shops in Evanston, Illinois. Mary works from 10:00 A.M. to 9:00 P.M. four days a week and 9:00 A.M. to 6:00 P.M. two days. She began her business with one employee in 1978; now she has a staff of twenty-three and plans to hire a business manager this year. Although she is certainly pleased with her success, Mary says that she has concentrated only on business for five years and that "now it is time to take care of me." That includes rethinking her growth objectives and enjoying the new house she bought last December.

The issue of how to handle unstructured time will be solved differently by different people in different lines of work, but most people need to spend a little time analyzing how they spend their day and then decide how much work needs to be done each week and how much personal time is needed. How to pace your new work life is your decision, for you are on your own every hour of your day and every day of your week.

Those Stressful First Few Months

After you have been self-employed for a few months, take the following brief quiz to see how well you are adjusting.

1. Do you frequently suffer from headaches, stomach pains, stiff back, or other physical discomfort?
 [] Yes [] No
2. Do you have trouble sleeping, or are you unable to sleep peacefully because of frequent vivid dreams about business problems?
 [] Yes [] No
3. Do you frequently skip meals, eat while you work, or wolf down your meals on the go?
 [] Yes [] No

4. Do you get angry easily and lose your temper frequently?
 [] Yes [] No
5. Do other people in business seem to have it relatively easy compared with you? Do they seem to get the lucky breaks while you have to work harder to get results?
 [] Yes [] No
6. Are you constantly thinking about business, even when watching TV, reading, or relaxing?
 [] Yes [] No
7. When talking with your spouse, friends, or relatives, do you steer the conversation toward business topics?
 [] Yes [] No
8. Do you sometimes feel that your spouse is not doing as much as you are to contribute to your family's income or financial future?
 [] Yes [] No

If you answered yes to three or more of these questions, you could be suffering from stress caused by the inability to separate work life from private life, a common problem among the newly self-employed.

Separating Work Time from Leisure Time

Having a personal life apart from work is vital to your mental health. Why? First, it allows you to relax and get away from the pressure of business. Even people who boast of being workaholics have suffered from burnout and nervous breakdowns.

Second, it is dangerous to invest *all* of your self-esteem in your business. If your work is your whole life, even minor business problems can send you into a depression. If you can balance your business activities with a healthy social and family life, you will be better able to put your work problems in perspective. When you have a life beyond the office, a business problem, no matter how serious, is not the end of your world.

Unfortunately, being self-employed is a demanding career, frequently much more so than working for someone else. You are wholly responsible for the success or failure of your enterprise, and running your own business makes enormous demands on your energy and time. But you should avoid becoming so absorbed in your work that you are unable to separate it from your personal life.

Here are some suggestions that can help you separate business activities from personal life and thus enjoy a more balanced existence.

Develop Steady Work Routines

- Before you stop working each day, make a list of unfinished tasks you must attend to tomorrow. Post this list on your bulletin board. Putting unfinished business items down on paper helps clear them from your mind.
- Try to finish any urgent or pressing task before you close the office for the day. Otherwise, it will be on your mind all evening.
- Change into different clothes after work, even if you don't have to.
- Set office hours, and stick to them as much as possible. Try to quit at a certain time each day.
- At the end of the day, clear your desk. Organize papers neatly in files, put the cover on the typewriter, empty the wastebasket, and drop the mail at the post office. This will give you a sense of having completed a day's work, and you will be less likely to worry about business after hours.

Establish Leisure Time Rules

- Is is necessary for you to be available to customers or clients on an emergency basis? If not, do not give them your home phone number, and do not carry a beeper.
- Do not bring work home if you can help it (even if your office is at home). If you have extra work to do, stay late in your office, or go in for a few hours on Saturday.

- Avoid doing work-related tasks after hours. For example, instead of reading a trade journal before dinner, try a novel instead so that you can truly relax and get your mind off business.

Learn Some Relaxation Techniques

- Take up a hobby or other activity, such as an exercise class, tennis, or gardening. These activities can help you enjoy your leisure and will take your mind off your work.
- Get involved in activities that are the opposite of what you do at work. For example, if you work indoors, spend your leisure time outdoors, perhaps hiking or driving in the country.
- Do not feel guilt about taking time off. You work hard, and you deserve a rest. There is nothing wrong or bad about watching TV, reading a book, or taking a nap.
- Do not try to combine work activities with relaxation. For example, do not try to write a report and watch TV at the same time. You will not get much work done, and you really will not be able to relax, either. Put the paper and pen away, grab a snack, sit back, and enjoy the show.

10

Bringing in the Business

GETTING YOUR FIRST CLIENT

We know a consultant who, when he was just starting out on his own, went to a career night at a local college. He asked one of the speakers how to create a flier for reaching training directors at large companies. The speaker told him how to put a flier together. Two weeks later, the consultant mailed a half-dozen fliers to training directors at insurance companies. The next week, he got a call from a large insurance company that eventually hired him to teach a seminar. He now has six insurance companies as clients, and he still cannot believe how successful that simple flier was.

The consultant was not highly experienced when he went out on his own, but he knew his field, he knew how to sell himself, and he was a good listener. In fact, when he went on his interview with the training director, he was about to ask for $1,500 for the seminar. But by listening closely to how the training director was discussing money, he knew instantly that $1,500 was too low. He doubled his price on the spot. The training director did not even blink.

A career consultant invested in a brochure and sent it to a number of personnel departments. As so often happens, the brochures floated from person to person. Eventually, she got

her first call. The person asked her to come in for an interview. The interviewer said he had "heard" that the career consultant was quite good. He hired her. It was her first job. The brochure had hit the desk of a harried executive who had been persuaded that the consultant must be a professional because her brochure was so professional.

These initial experiences demonstrate that attitude and presentation are the clinchers in getting your business started, not a wealth of experience and some friends in the business. Here are a few tips on gaining and keeping your first client.

1. *Be a pro right from the start.* Whether you have zero experience or years in the field, present yourself as a professional. That means dressing well, investing in professional-looking literature about your company, and giving a personal touch to every contact you make with every prospect.

2. *Try everything.* Clients can be found by sharing a taxi and discussing what you do, across a dinner table, through cold phone calls. They *can* be found, but you have to believe deeply in what you are selling and in your prospect's need to buy it.

3. *References are nice, but not crucial.* Very few people take the time to check references. You may use a reference: teachers, friends in managerial positions, or even relatives in managerial positions. Demonstrate your talents by practicing on people, and they can be your first references.

4. *Do not worry if your academic credentials do not reflect your current field.* One of the authors, Gary Blake, holds a Ph.D. in theater. This did not deter him from establishing himself, in his mid-thirties, as a business writing consultant. Few people have ever asked Gary just what his Ph.D. is in. As a matter of fact, Gary has autographed his books at dozens of bookstores and has never once been asked by a store manager to prove that he was, indeed, Gary Blake. People are more trusting than you might imagine.

5. *Work for free if you have to.* No one will ask if you got paid when you did work for a client, so you may want to take on a few *pro bono* clients who can help bolster your credentials. You will not get rich, but you will at least be building a client list.

6. *It is better to work for a little money than not to work at all.* When it comes to getting your first client or customer, take whatever comes your way, even if it is for minimal pay. The important thing is to get that first client under your belt to establish yourself in the field. Experience is what you are after now. Big bucks can come later.

FINDING NEW CLIENTS

Few free-lancers or entrepreneurs are so overwhelmed with business that a little more would not help. Sure, you may be able to look ahead for six months and say, "I could not accept any more business if I wanted it!" But things will eventually quiet down, and you will have to prime the pump again.

When things slow down, return to basics. Ask yourself the same old questions: Who needs your product or service? What are the age, education, and income of your best customers? Where do they shop? What do they read? What are the geographic boundaries of your market? How did your customers come to you in the past? Where have your most effective ads been placed?

Here are a few time-tested techniques for bringing in new business.

Fliers and Brochures

Fliers are handbills that can be created and distributed inexpensively. Where you distribute handbills depends on your business. The founder of Access International wanted to reach college students to tell them about their company's low

charter flight rates to Europe. The two owners, Paris Themmen and Yale Brozen, buy unsold seats for charter flights and sell them at tremendous discounts. They reach students by posting fliers on lampposts and bulletin boards near colleges.

A small law firm put posters and handbills in a building where apartments were about to be sold, making the lawyers visible to a group of people who needed landlord-tenant advice.

Most photocopy stores have bulletin boards that carry fliers, business cards, and announcements of a number of neighborhood businesses. Some self-employed people thrive on this type of free advertising, and many small businesses have been launched with this exposure. These bulletin boards are useful for finding new customers for movers, typing services, word processing centers, boutiques, accountants, tax preparers, contractors, dog walkers, artists, photographers, personal computer consultants, and many others.

Brochures, on the other hand, are more durable, more expensive to produce, and more impressive than fliers. A brochure presents your company's products or services in a thorough, structured way. It may also give some background on your company, a list of clients, and some information about the people who run the company. Executive recruiters, consultants, engineering firms, and many other businesses interested in making an impression find it worthwhile to produce a company brochure. Many produce separate brochures for each product or service they offer.

Mailings

Direct mail and sales letters can also help you find customers. Computer consultants might want to send a letter to vice presidents of information systems at large companies; a training consultant can write to training directors; free-lance researchers might write to authors, editors, and publishers.

Mailings can be expensive. After all, every letter you send requires a stamp, an envelope, and a letterhead as well as the brochure you enclose. Yet, if you are selling a high-priced product, even a small response rate, 1 or 2 percent, can more than justify the cost.

Mailing list brokers are listed in the Yellow Pages. Call several of them, and ask for their catalogs. Then compare the prices of the lists that are most appropriate for your needs.

Special Promotions

A wide variety of businesses make use of special promotions. Theater groups often circulate discount tickets to shops and markets in the neighborhood. Bruce Jordan and Marilyn Abrams, producers of *Shear Madness,* Boston's longest-running play, did a wide variety of special promotions to find new audiences for their show. They handed out complimentary tickets to merchants and hotel employees, people who would spread the word. They also distributed "play money" ("In Entertainment We Trust"), offering $2 discounts on their already low ticket prices. These gimmicks worked. Dozens of successful theater companies are now performing the play.

Mrs. Fields, the chocolate chip cookie entrepreneur, started her business by walking along the sidewalk and handing out samples of her cookies. Dr. William Scholl also used the direct approach to sell items like arch supports. Scholl would walk into a shoe store, produce a skeleton of the human foot, toss it on the counter in front of the startled proprietor, and proceed to discuss the foot's anatomy. At the conclusion of his talk, he would pitch his Foot-Eazer; the manager almost invariably placed an order for the product.

A bookstore owner offered the following ideas for stimulating new bookstore business: free drawings using the names and addresses of patrons, preferred-customer dis-

counts, posting fliers in libraries, knowing which authors Phil Donahue would be featuring on upcoming shows and then doing a window display of those authors' books.

Luncheons and Parties

These social events can bring new people to your door. Such enjoyable promotions are unthreatening to the prospective customer and allow you to soft-sell your product or service. A deluxe restaurant could gain media attention by hosting a charity affair. A wine and cheese party could help attract people to a new boutique.

When two women opened a new women's apparel shop in a small New York State town, they were faced with the challenge of attracting customers from other towns within a twenty-mile radius. They wanted to send out invitations to introduce people to their store. The problem, however, was obtaining a good list of prospects. So they invited friends from the town to a luncheon. Ten women dined and provided five hundred names and addresses of friends and acquaintances. Those names became a permanent part of the shop's mailing list.

Telemarketing

Selling on the phone can be effective for certain types of businesses. A consultant might not be able to telemarket his or her services without seeming hungry, but investment counselors have found clients by calling affluent people and offering to sell them tax shelters.

Business Gifts, Premiums, and Giveaways

In an effort to keep your name in front of your clients, you may want to devise a giveaway or premium. Insurance

companies give their clients calendars. A gift store may give its customers pens. Ideally, these gifts are inexpensive, tasteful, and linked to the type of business you are in.

Newsletters

Newsletters are printed sheets or small newspapers that contain information of interest to a particular group. Generally, they are mailed to a regular list of paying or nonpaying subscribers and are published on a regular basis: daily, weekly, monthly, or quarterly. In recent years, newsletters have become a popular form of communication, primarily because they are concise, easy to read, focused, and inexpensive to produce.

Trade Shows

A trade show is a gathering of people from the same industry. If you sell products to highly specific markets, such as engineers, doctors, chemical plants, or restaurant owners, concentrate on trade shows. The reference book *Trade Shows and Professional Exhibits Directory* (Detroit: Gale Research) provides details on more than 2,100 scheduled exhibitions, trade shows, association conventions, and other events organized to facilitate direct sales and trade contacts. Trade shows offer opportunities to give a presentation, hand out brochures and business cards, pick up competitors' literature, and meet prospects.

You will, of course, devise other ways of reaching your new clients, from print advertising (newspapers, magazines, classified sections, display, Yellow Pages) to signs, billboards, and posters.

Once you get in the habit of being promotion-minded, you will never be at a loss for new ways to build your business.

GAINING RECOGNITION

It is not enough to create a new company and offer a superior product or service. You will not win customers or clients unless people *know* about your business, your product, or your service. One affordable way to gain recognition is through publicity and public relations.

What are publicity and public relations? And how do they differ from paid advertising? In a recent newspaper interview, Lee Solters, publicist for Frank Sinatra and Barbra Streisand, defines his business this way:

> When the circus comes to town and you paint a sign about it, that's advertising. Put the sign on the back of an elephant and march him through town, that's promotion. If the elephant walks through the mayor's flower bed, that's publicity. And if you can get the mayor to laugh or comment about it—that's public relations!

In this section, we will look at some of the ways you can use publicity and public relations to gain visibility for your new business venture.

Public Speaking

According to speech writer Joseph J. Kelley, Jr., at least 5 million speeches are delivered annually in the United States. Of this number, 1 million are given by businesspeople, people much like yourself.

Why are these folks being asked to speak? Because each has unique knowledge and experience that others may benefit from hearing about. And so do you. For example, if you run a home improvement business, you are an expert in two areas people are curious about: home improvements and running your own business.

As a businessperson, you can talk about careers in your field. Or how to start your own business. Or what the

consumer should look for when buying your type of product or service. Or how to gain skill in your trade or profession.

Here are some lecture topics the self-employed home contractor could speak about.

- How to Start and Run Your Own Home Improvement Business
- Twenty-five Common Home Improvements and What You Can Expect to Pay for Them
- Your Career in Home Improvements
- How to Protect Yourself Against Dishonest Home Improvement Contractors
- Ten Questions to Ask Before You Hire a Contractor
- Eight Easy Home Repairs and How to Do Them Right
- How to Maintain Your Home on Only $100 a Month

See how easily a list of useful topics can be culled from the speaker's general background. And this list does not begin to explore more specific topics, such as how to build an extra room, how to finish your basement, how to make your own plumbing repairs, and how to add a dormer.

Does the businessperson speak for money? Not primarily, although some organizations do pay speakers. The businessperson's main purposes in giving talks are to become known to potential clients and customers and to gain greater visibility and prominence in the industry and community.

How do you get speaking engagements? You may be invited to speak to a church, school, or community group or at a social club, professional society, or trade association. By all means, accept the invitation, and deliver the speech. You may be asked back if your speech is successful. People in the audience may spread the word about you. Soon you may receive other invitations to lecture.

If you do not get asked to speak, you can always solicit speaking invitations. Send a letter offering your services as a speaker to groups before which you would like to appear. In the letter, state your topic, briefly outline the speech, tell

what the audience will get out of it, and say that you are available. Do not ask for money; be willing to speak just for the publicity and exposure.

Teaching

Teaching a course offers another opportunity to become visible in your community. You will not reach as large an audience as you would on the lecture circuit, but the real publicity value of teaching is that it establishes you as an expert in your field. Even today's skeptical society has a certain respect for teachers and professors.

You do not have to be a teacher by profession to teach a class. Businesspeople, valued for the real-life experience they bring to the academic world, teach all sorts of business and technical courses, from computer programming and statistical analysis to marketing, selling, advertising, and promotion. Where do they teach? In community colleges, business schools, and adult education programs.

If you have a hankering to get up in front of the chalkboard, write to the dean of a nearby business school or college. Propose a course, and describe your qualifications to teach it. You may be wearing a professor's hat before you know it.

If you do not get invited to teach a course or give a lecture, you can create your own speaking event: a public seminar. To do this, you will need to rent a hall or hotel room, pick a date, and announce the seminar through advertising and direct mail or by distributing notices and fliers.

Your seminar can be about any topic. The only requirements are that (1) you have enough expertise to deliver a meaningful talk, (2) your topic is of sufficient interest to attract an audience, (3) you have sufficient public speaking skill to hold the audience's attention, and (4) the seminar will

help promote you, your business, or the product or service you offer.

Unless you are wealthy enough to foot the hotel and advertising bills, you should charge people a fee to attend the seminar. The fee you set depends on what people are willing to pay and how much money you hope to make from the seminar. Some entrepreneurs turn their seminars into activities that are profitable in themselves; others are content to break even on seminars, knowing the seminars are valuable for the publicity they bring.

Writing

Another way to build your reputation and get visibility is to write articles or books.

Articles

The publicity benefits of article writing are twofold: First, writing articles quickly establishes you as an expert in your field, much as teaching does. Articles reach a far broader audience, however; many trade publications are read by thousands of people. Second, reprints of your article make excellent sales literature.

What can you write about? Pretty much any subject on which you consider yourself an expert and in which readers of industry journals would be interested. If a topic makes a good speech, it will probably make a good article, too. A home contractor, for example, might write an article comparing different insulation materials and then submit it for publication to a contracting or trade magazine.

Pick a magazine in which you would like to be published. Read a few issues, and then come up with a topic you think would appeal to the magazine's readers. Send a query letter to the editor proposing the topic; outline the contents of the

article and your credentials in the field. If the editor responds to your letter and asks for the article, go ahead and write it. If you get turned down, retype your query letter, and sent it to another publication.

For complete instructions on how to write and publish articles, see *How to Write Articles That Sell,* by L. Perry Wilbur (New York: John Wiley & Sons, 1981).

Books

If an article impresses people, a book with your name on it is bound to impress them even more. "The reverence people have for the printed word is amazing," writes publisher Edward Uhlan in his autobiography, *The Rogue of Publishers' Row* (Smithtown, NY: Exposition Press, 1956). "Simply because a man appears in print, the public assumes that he has something authoritative to say."

Are you an expert on some business or technical topic? Do people want to know about that topic enough to buy a book on it? Then perhaps you can sell your book idea to a publisher.

It's a good idea to create an outline, a proposal describing the book idea, and a sample chapter or two and then to show this material to publishers. This saves you the trouble of writing a book if no publisher is interested. A good book proposal clearly explains, in just a few pages, what the book is about, who the potential readers are, and why they should want to read it. The proposal also points out ways in which your book is different from and better than other books on the topic.

We recommend that you find a literary agent who, for 10 or 15 percent of the money, will try to sell your book to a publisher. A good agent has many contacts in the publishing world and therefore has a better chance of selling your book than you do. A reputable agent gets paid only when the sale is made. Avoid any agent who asks for a reading fee, editing fee, critique fee, or any other payment up front. Also be

aware that many agents are not interested in talking with unpublished authors. You may have to try a few before you come to one who will consider your proposal.

NETWORKING

Networking is a new name for an activity that has been going on for a long time: doing business through personal contacts. The purpose of networking is to meet as many people as possible who can help you in some way. And the reason these other people are networking is to find someone who can help them—perhaps you.

In *Success* magazine (July/August 1985), Steve Fishman wrote that networking is "the single-minded pursuit of useful contacts at every convention, seminar, or neighborhood barbecue. To the networker, every stranger represents an opportunity, the chance to find prospects, reach targets, or meet friends."

Business Builder or Time Waster?

A great many people swear by networking; however, an equal number of people swear *at* it. Many self-employed people have told us that they get a great deal of new business from the contacts they make while networking; some get the *majority* of their clients this way. Others insist that advertising, direct mail, publicity, and word of mouth are far more effective methods of building business and that the time spent going to meetings and networking parties would be better spent doing moneymaking work for current clients.

Will networking be a business builder or a time waster for you? The only way to know for sure is to try it and see.

Networking in Action

Jon is an account executive with a public relations firm specializing in high-tech accounts. His job is to get his cli-

ents—computer manufacturers, software publishers, and other high-tech businesses—written up in the newspapers and the trade press and talked about on radio and television.

Jon attends a dinner meeting of a local computer society, not for the meal, but to network. During the social hour before dinner, Jon sets out to meet and speak with as many people as possible.

First he meets Carol, who has just taken a position as associate editor with an important computer magazine. Carol expresses interest in doing a story on a new computer chip manufactured by one of Jon's clients. Jon promises to send background information to Carol, and they exchange cards.

Next, Jon overhears a conversation between two executives. One is complaining about how the computer press has ignored his company's new, innovative software products. Jon introduces himself, and the executive perks up. He says he would like to know more about how Jon's firm could help him get better press coverage. They exchange cards, and Jon promises to call tomorrow to arrange an appointment.

Jon then talks to Phil, a technical writer specializing in computer manuals. Phil complains that business is slow, and Jon remembers that his agency needs someone to ghostwrite a speech for a client. He offers Phil the job. Phil says he will stop by Jon's office on Wednesday to discuss the project in detail.

Within thirty minutes, Jon has made three contacts: a possible placement for a story, a potential new client, and a writer to handle a pressing project. And he is just getting started.

How to Network

Here are some tips that can help you network effectively.

1. *Put yourself into the network mode.* When you step into the room, switch your gears from passive to active. People are

not going to come running to you; you must introduce yourself to them. Do not be shy; networking requires aggressiveness.

2. *Probe for information.* You find out about the other person by asking questions: "What do you do?" "Who are you with?" "Do you know [a certain person, a company, a product]?" "Tell me more about your business." This way, networkers quickly determine whether a contact can pay off.

3. *Do not sell while networking.* Your purpose is to make contacts, not get an order. The hard-sell approach is inappropriate. In conversation, try to learn all you can about the other people—their wants, interests, needs, problems. Later on, you can try to solve those problems and fill those needs.

4. *Exchange cards.* Carry an ample supply of business cards, and keep them handy in a pocket or purse. Never end a promising conversation without exchanging cards.

5. *Follow up within two weeks.* Follow up on promising leads by mail and phone. And do it soon, while the memory of the meeting is still fresh in your contact's mind. Also, make it a habit to periodically send short letters, article clippings, or informal notes to people you have met while networking.

6. *Organize your contact file.* Those business cards you collect are precious resources; lose them or misplace them, and you lose your contacts. Buy a plastic card-filing system for holding and organizing your collection (alphabetical order by name is best). Or you may want to transfer these names to a floppy disk and store your contacts in a computer data base.

7. *Edit your card file.* To prevent your network of contacts from becoming too large to manage, periodically weed out those that are of no use.

8. *Know your limits.* Some people thrive on networking. Others find it a necessary but exhausting task. Limit your own networking to a comfortable level so that you do not feel burned out. You cannot network effectively if your mind is focused on getting out, getting home, and going to sleep.

Networking Opportunities

Where do you network? At any meeting or gathering where potential clients, colleagues, employees, employers, and other contacts are likely to be in attendance. Some of these places include:

- Trade associations
- Professional societies
- Churches
- Community organizations
- Local business clubs and groups

In addition, you might consider participating in select groups on a more regular basis. The annual membership fee for most trade and professional associations ranges from $20 to $100. This investment can pay for itself rapidly in networking contacts.

11

Money and Success

CREDIT AND COLLECTION

Whether you offer a product or a service, you will probably allow your customers and clients to buy on credit. And when you extend credit, you take the risk of having your bills paid late or not at all.

It is true that only a small percentage of clients are deadbeats. But an increasing number are paying bills late. Large corporations in particular make it standard operating procedure to pay their vendors (who are often small, entrepreneurial firms) one to four months after service is rendered.

Late payments and unpaid bills can create a serious cash crunch for the independent professional or small business. At any time, between 10 to 70 percent of your total wealth will be tied up in outstanding debt. If the bills are not paid, you will have a hard time meeting your own obligations, and your business could be in danger of going under.

Although bookkeeping may be boring, collecting unpaid bills is as important as making a sale. You make no profit on a job until the client's check clears in your account.

Smart Credit

By extending credit, you are in effect giving your customer or client an interest-free loan, but credit is smart business for most entrepreneurs. You must be competitive in the marketplace, and most clients and customers will not buy from a firm that does not extend credit.

The goal of your credit policy is not to eliminate the risk of nonpayment—that is impossible—but to reduce it by being careful about the people to whom you give credit and about the way you give it.

Here are some tips to help you be smarter about credit.

Check Out the Customer

The character of the customer will determine whether the person can be trusted to pay a bill. First impressions do help. Does the person come across as honest, or does your gut instinct warn you against him or her? If you are uncomfortable with extending credit to a person, you can simply insist on getting all or part of the money up front.

When selling to individuals, be aware of what makes for a good credit risk and what does not. Stability is the sign of a good credit risk. Favor the customer who owns a home, has a steady income, and has lived in the community for many years. Family people make better credit risks than singles. People with a lot of insurance, stocks, bonds, investments, and credit cards are also good risks. Beware of people who lack roots. Those who switch jobs frequently and move often are greater risks because they can easily pull up stakes and run away from outstanding debt.

If you are selling to businesses, the size and reputation of the firm are important. A Fortune 500 client is likely to be good for the money, but small start-up companies are a greater risk. Check the Dun & Bradstreet credit rating of the firm to be sure.

Ask for credit references: two companies the client deals

with and the name of the client's bank. Call the references, and ask what their experience has been with the client.

Put It in Writing

Put the terms of the business agreement in a purchase order, letter, or contract, and get it signed by the client before you deliver products or begin to perform a service. On large, complex jobs, you may want to submit a detailed proposal outlining schedule, fees, and method of billing.

If possible, get 50 percent up front on the first order. Make a photocopy of the first check you receive from the client, and save it. This gives you a permanent record of the bank where the client keeps his or her checking account. This information can be valuable if you have to take the client to court later on.

Educate Your Customers

Explain your credit and billing policy in detail when you accept an order. Let the client know how you bill and when bills will be sent. The clients should never be surprised by any bills or credit-related correspondence they receive from you.

Do not allow any one client to build up a large debt. If the client has invoices outstanding, insist that the overdue bills be paid before you accept additional orders on credit.

Provide Incentives for Prompt Payment

Consider adding a monthly interest charge, known as a *late charge*, to overdue bills. This is an incentive to pay on time. You might also offer a discount (typically 2 to 5 percent) to people who pay promptly—say, within ten days.

Send an occasional letter to good payers thanking them for paying their bills on time. This gives people the motivation to continue to pay on time to preserve their good record with you.

Collection Tips and Techniques

No matter how careful you are, a small percentage of your clients will not pay their bills on time. Here are some proven ways to get your bills paid while preserving the goodwill of valued customers.

Start Dunning Right Away

Begin collection action the instant the bill becomes overdue. Do not allow bills to remain unpaid. The longer a debt is outstanding, the less chance you have of collecting it.

Your first action should be to send a polite letter requesting payment. Do not take an angry or abusive tone. Assume that the client intended to pay but that there was a clerical foul-up somewhere. The first collection letter is a reminder, not an accusation. Do not forget to state the date and amount of the invoice due, what it was for, and when you expect payment.

Be Persistent

If you get no response within two or three weeks, send another reminder letter. Be polite but a little firmer.

Do not let up after the second letter. Keep the letters coming to show the client that paying the bill is important and that you will not forget about the invoice.

Send letters by certified mail, return receipt requested. This proves to a court that the client did in fact receive your mail. It can also scare people into paying their bills.

Use the Telephone

Telephone calls are appropriate after the third letter. Again, be polite but firm. Do not lose your cool, and do not get emotional or personal. An outburst rarely wins cooperation.

Inform the client that you will take legal action if the bill is not paid; but beyond that, do not threaten the debtor in any

call or letter. Making threats to collect bills is illegal and may result in a lawsuit against you.

In collection letters and calls, remind the customer that he or she *signed an order* for the goods or services delivered. The client's personal signature on that order creates a stronger obligation to pay.

Get Them to Respond

If you cannot get payment in full, try for partial payment and a signed promise to pay the rest according to a schedule you and the client can agree to.

Watch out for partial-payment checks that have "payment in full" or a similar message written on them. If you cash the check, it becomes, in effect, a new contract between you and the client and cancels the remainder of the debt.

If you cannot get even partial payment, at least try to get the customer to send you a letter indicating an intent to pay. This forces him or her to take the debt seriously and will also be useful when and if you go to court.

Save all paper work connected with the goods delivered or the job performed and the collection action, including photocopies of any checks received, a telephone log record of all phone conversations, and copies of all correspondence between you and the client. Documentation can make or break your case before a judge.

Some Other Techniques

If you have a personal relationship with the debtor, appeal to his or her sense of fair play and honesty. Try to deal with the person who writes the checks, rather than with an underling. Assistants and administrators are usually powerless to take action.

Send monthly statements to the debtor. They provide a regular reminder to clients that bills are outstanding.

Consider cutting off further product delivery or service until the overdue invoice is paid.

Attorneys and Collection Agencies

If you become disgusted, or if the effort to collect is unpleasant or takes too much of your time and energy, you can use the services of a collection agency or attorney. These people usually work on a contingency basis; their fee will be from 10 to 40 percent of the amount they collect for you.

Before you turn the collection money over to the agency or attorney, you might pay a lawyer to send one more collection letter, on his or her letterhead, to the debtor. A collection letter on an attorney's stationery can often frighten a debtor into paying, and most attorneys charge only $25 to $75 for writing such a letter.

For invoices ranging from $500 to $1,500 (depending on the laws of your state), you may be able to take the case to small claims court. No lawyer is needed for this.

Settlements

If the debtor offers to settle for an amount below what is owed, accept only as a last resort. You deserve to be paid in full, and you should be. However, you must weigh the settlement offer against the time and expense of taking further collection action. Sometimes, it is best to accept a settlement offer just to be rid of the whole thing.

Maintain goodwill after the debt is paid. In time, the debtor may become a good customer again. However, you should insist on a stricter credit policy on all future dealings because of past experience.

THE DREADED QUARTERLY TAX PAYMENTS

Paying taxes is rather easy when you work for someone else. Your employer simply withholds the appropriate federal, state, and city taxes from your pay. The check you receive represents the money you have earned *after* taxes.

At the end of the year, you or your accountant computes your taxes. Depending on your situation, you may end up owing some extra taxes, or you may get a refund. But chances are the amount you owe is usually pretty close to the amount your employer withheld and paid to the tax collectors for you during the year.

For self-employed people, the situation is quite different. Clients or customers pay you for the full amount and do not withhold taxes from the check or cash they give you. *You* are responsible for paying income tax, sales tax, and other taxes that may be owed on this income.

Does this mean you get to keep all the money until you file your income tax returns on April 15? Unfortunately, no. Self-employed people are required to make partial payments to Uncle Sam and to the state and local tax authorities based on their best estimate of what their income will be. Most of us make these payments on a quarterly basis.

Help from Your Accountant

Your accountant can examine your records and advise you on how much you should pay each quarter, when to pay, and where to send your payments. He or she can also provide the special forms or payment vouchers required. Most self-employed people make four quarterly payments, which are due on April 15, June 15, September 15, and January 15.

At the end of the year, you add up your income, then subtract your expenses to determine your profit. The actual amount you owe the Internal Revenue Service is based on this profit. If you made more than you originally estimated, you probably owe the IRS some money. But if you made less than anticipated, you may receive a refund. Again, your accountant is the one to figure this out for you.

It is a good idea to add up your income and expenses and calculate your profits before you make your payments for

each quarter. Call your accountant, and tell him or her how much you have made. Your accountant may suggest that you raise or lower your quarterly payment, depending on whether you are earning more or less than you originally projected. By doing this, you ensure that your quarterly payments are in line with your actual income. This way, there are no surprises come April 15.

If you do not monitor your income and adjust your quarterly payments accordingly, you could earn far more income than the figure on which your quarterly payments were based. If that happens, you could be required to make an extremely large payment to the IRS when you file your returns; and that can be upsetting, especially if you do not have the cash on hand. Moreover, if your payments fall below a certain percentage of what you should have been paying, the IRS can tack a penalty charge onto your tax bill.

Coping with Quarterly Tax Payments

As a self-employed person, you must get used to the fact that you cannot keep all the money you earn. It is easy to lull yourself into a false sense of wealth by thinking that you are $5,000 richer when you receive a $5,000 check from a client. But in fact, you are not $5,000 richer. If you are in a 50 percent tax bracket, you are only $2,500 richer. The other $2,500 belongs to the federal, state, and city governments, not to you.

Therefore, when you receive payments, plan your budget with this fact in mind. Do not go out and spend your income as you receive it; otherwise you will have trouble making your tax payments later in the year.

One method of budgeting for tax payments is to mentally divide all business income in half—half for you and half for Uncle Sam. You can spend your half, but do not touch Uncle Sam's. This ensures that you will have money to pay Uncle

Sam when he wants it. (People below the 50 percent tax bracket might set aside a third or fourth of their business income for Uncle Sam, depending on what bracket they are in.)

Another method is to make sure you have enough money in your bank account to cover your quarterly payment. Even better, save enough money to cover the next *two* payments. This way, you will worry less when those due dates come up.

Getting Over the Shock

Many free-lancers and entrepreneurs go into shock the first time they learn about quarterly estimated tax payments, and that is only natural. Except for buying a home or a car, you will rarely plunk down as much money for a single item as you will pay to meet your quarterly obligations to the IRS and your local tax authorities.

For example, if you are self-employed and think you will be earning $80,000 *net* income (your income after expenses), you will have to come up with $5,790 every three months for your estimated federal tax payments. (This figure is based on the 1985 IRS tax schedule for a married, self-employed individual filing jointly with his or her spouse. It does not include payments toward Social Security, which come to an additional $1,168 per quarter. And depending on where you live, there may be state and city taxes, too.)

Unless you are wealthy, this is a lot of money to shell out four times a year. And it hurts even more because many taxpayers seem to feel that they get nothing in return. When you write a large check to a department store, you receive all sorts of luxury items in return: rugs, furs, jewelry, gourmet food, furniture, fine china, a stereo, a VCR, anything your heart desires. But when you write a check for taxes, it seems to disappear—poof!—into the air.

Of course, this is not true. Your tax dollars go toward

running the country and the state. They *do* give you services in return: public education, roadways, garbage collection, sewage systems. But many people just do not see it this way, and they resent the big bite taxes take out of their income. This bite, which is taken in tiny nibbles from workers' weekly paychecks, seems more burdensome to the self-employed person, who must write huge checks for it every three months.

Paying estimated taxes will probably never be pleasant for you. But if you plan wisely, you won't feel the bite as badly. And as time goes by, you will get used to the idea. Believe us, the first year is the worst.

SHAKING THE MONEY TREE: HOW TO RAISE YOUR FEES

There will come a time when you must raise your fees or prices. Perhaps your suppliers have raised their prices, maybe inflation is rampant, or perhaps your growth—in education, stature, or experience—merits an increase in pay.

Here are examples of how two self-employed businesspeople raised their fees.

Architect on the Spot

An architect offering design services to small businesses charges by the job. Most of his clients are contractors and small-business owners who have small budgets for services such as designing track lighting or drawing floor plans. The architect customarily charges $500 to help small businesses design a track lighting system and figure out where shelves can be built. One day, however, this architect gets a call from an individual in another town. The prospective client wants him to design a music room for his home, a mansion on a hill. He has heard about the architect's work from a friend. As he describes the type of music room he wants, the

architect realizes that the budget for this project is "whatever it takes to complete it."

The architect also realizes that this project will stretch his talents. He sees that it is of a different order than jobs he has done in the past. He recognizes that his responsibilities will be great and that this project is a one-shot deal; in other words, he probably will not be getting more work in the future from this particular customer. He names a fee higher than what he has charged in the past. The client accepts it without hesitation. "Now," says the new client, "when can you begin work?"

This is a situational price hike. The architect seized a rare opportunity to complete a special project, and he raised his fee on the spot. He did so for three reasons: First, he was dealing directly with a person who obviously had an ample budget. Second, the architect realized that the project called for more than the usual amount of effort and hence merited higher than normal pay. Third, he sensed that he had no competition. Other people could, of course, be found to do the job; but given the special circumstances of the appointment, he was not in direct competition with anyone. Almost any fee he named, within reason, would have been acceptable to an affluent person eager to solve a pressing problem.

It turned out that the architect was right. Of course, things could have turned out differently. The prospective client could have said, "Most architects charge less for this type of work. Why is your fee so high?" The architect could then have improvised an answer or lowered his price. However, neither would have been an impressive strategy because the customer would probably have been left with the feeling that the architect had tried to overcharge him.

A Therapist Gives Notice

A psychologist tells each patient, at an apt moment, that her fee will rise from $45 an hour to $55, beginning in Septem-

ber, six weeks away. Knowing that this may present difficulty for several of her patients, she explains her reasons for the rate increase and offers to discuss the matter.

Tips on Raising Your Fees or Prices

An increase in fees is never good news. But you can make it less unpleasant by giving the client a chance to get used to the idea. When you have to raise your fees, let people know six weeks to three months in advance. Also, give your reasons, even if you do not really have to do so. People appreciate knowing why they will be paying more. The better your reasons, the less chance your customers will challenge a price hike.

When you increase your rates, it may seem cataclysmic to the person who needs your product or service and is at the same time short of cash. But if you believe it is fair to raise your fees across the board, go ahead and do so; just be sympathetic to clients with financial problems.

Any price hike can seem like a shakedown, a challenge to pay up or stop being served. To lower the anxiety level of your customers, you will want to raise fees in the most businesslike and least painful manner. Here are some suggestions.

Give a Reason for the Increase

Customers are human. They may not like a price hike but they can learn to live with it if they are made to see that the increase is both reasonable and necessary.

Do Not Raise Your Fees Too Much

It is hard enough to get your customers to accept a small rate hike. Do not add insult to injury by raising your fees through the roof. Keep increases no higher than 20 percent, so that

they will be in keeping with the rise in the cost of living. If you double or triple your fees, you may lose all your clients, especially if there are lower-priced competitors ready to take your place.

Sometimes it is wise to experiment by raising your fee with a new client. By simply telling a prospect of your new fee, without pointing out that it is higher than it has been, you can see how price-sensitive your product or service is. If the new client accepts the price, you can then consider raising the fees with other clients. However, if the new client seems upset with the fee you quote, you may conclude that an increase is not yet in order.

Raise Fees for Special Services or Products

A speech writer told us about a phone call he received from a corporate vice president who asked about the cost of a ten-page speech. After some discussion about the subject matter and other specifications, the speech writer quoted a fee of $2,000. The vice president agreed readily. "When can I get it?" he asked. "When do you need it?" asked the writer, expecting he would have a month to do the writing. "By this weekend," said the vice president. The speech writer, after an astonished pause, said, "The weekend is only three days away. I usually require three or four weeks to write the type of speech you have described. I could do it, but it would mean working day and night. It would also mean that you would have to be available to answer my questions all the time. I would do revisions on the spot. But I would have to charge you an extra $500, and I would need the fee paid in advance."

The vice president was put off by the higher price, even though it was justified by the circumstances. He was also a bit miffed at the request for advance payment.

The speech writer, however, had several excellent reasons for demanding a higher fee and advance payment. First, he

did not know the caller and had never done business with him or with his firm. Second, he did not expect the caller to become a regular client. As he saw it, this was to be a difficult one-shot project. Third, he felt that if the vice president could demand extra-fast work, he had the right to demand extra payment and to protect himself by requesting that it be paid in advance.

At first, the vice president turned down the speech writer's request. But he called back an hour later and accepted the offer. Why? He simply had not realized that unusual circumstances merit unusual working conditions and higher pay. He had called three other writers, all of whom said they would not write the speech in three days for any amount of money.

Don't Look Back

Raising prices strengthens those risk-taking muscles that self-employed people must keep toned up. Once you have taken action, do not waiver or haggle or get involved in discussions about how high your fees are. There will always be someone who can offer a product or service at a lower price. If you think your fees may be perceived as too high, just remember the words of painter James McNeill Whistler. He was once asked how he could charge several hundred dollars for a painting that took him less than a day to complete. Whistler replied, "You are not paying for my time; you are paying for a lifetime of sensitivity."

MONITORING YOUR PROGRESS

Running a business without periodically monitoring your progress is like steering a ship without looking at the compass. Measuring your profitability as well as the success of your marketing effort is crucial to make the decisions that will take your enterprise from the survival stage to the

growth stage. As in scientific research, the experiments that don't work are often as valuable as those that do because they tell you what not to do in the future.

We devote most of this section to monitoring your marketing effort because in the early stages of self-employment, reaching customers is all-important. At the end of the section, we will give you a checklist of other items to be monitored. They include growth, profitability, customer satisfaction, tax planning, the industry, and your personal satisfaction.

Keeping track of your marketing promotions teaches you what works and what does not. Recordkeeping lets you know that a bad month need not mean that your business is about to die; it may reflect an industrywide lull or some other partly predictable situation. By monitoring your business closely, you can begin to focus your efforts on those tactics that have been successful. You can then plan the future so that the normal ups and downs of business will not keep you on a roller coaster of anxiety.

Personal computers have revolutionized the recordkeeping procedures of many small businesses. By creating data bases that track the progress of certain facets of your business, you can better control information, and you can make decisions based on better-ordered and more complete sets of data than ever before. At the touch of a key, you can call up data bases that show your monthly gross or expenses, your inventory, a list of prospects to contact, or your income by client.

You also can track expenses by category and thus catch fluctuations. You can tell how much you have spent on printing or electricity or photocopying. The longer you stay in business and the better records you keep, the better chance you have of remaining in business because you will have removed much of the uncertainty from your day-to-day operations.

Whether you use a computer or an old-fashioned ledger,

you will find that marketing takes recordkeeping to an extreme. By using statistics, demographics, surveys, and questionnaires, large marketing concerns can describe a product or service's market down to the number of cavities in each customer's teeth. But for your purposes, you should keep detailed records of the results of each promotion you do in the never-ending quest to find ways to increase your business. Don't trust your memory. Keep records of inquiries, and group those inquiries in a variety of ways: by industry, location, or perhaps size of company. Remember that inquiries are meaningless unless they result in sales. You will find that certain advertising or promotional vehicles will result in fewer inquiries but higher rates of sales per inquiry. It takes a keen eye to watch for and note these situations.

Measuring the results of promotions shows you the most cost-effective ways to reach customers. It can give you options. Is it wise to spend three hours a day making cold calls if little business has come in from the effort? Would it be better to use a direct mail program? You might get fewer inquiries, but each one could be a better lead than those derived from cold calls. Should you spend a large amount of money on an ad that will reach thousands of prospects at relatively little money per prospect, even though some of those prospects will live in areas remote from your place of business? These are some questions to ask yourself; the answers, naturally, will vary from business to business.

You can never stop testing. You cannot know what sales and marketing methods will work until you try them. And if you spend money trying something, you owe it to yourself to be meticulous in recording, with scientific detail, how well that technique works for you.

When you do find a promotion that works, you may be able to use it many times with no loss of success and with no decline in the number of inquiries it produces.

After you have been in business for several years, you will begin to spot the trends in your business and in your promo-

tions. By spotting trends, you give yourself lead time in which to respond to negative trends and capitalize on perceived opportunities.

Here are a few questions that year-by-year monitoring should answer.

1. Has your business grown in sales each year? Has it increased in profitability? Do you have more clients or customers? How profitable is each client?

2. Which promotions work best for your business? Ads? Word of mouth? Publicity? Phone calls? Personal selling? Direct mail?

3. Which months or seasons are slow? Which are usually busy? What accounts for the cycle? Which months are the best for advertising? For sending out direct mail packages?

4. Has your marketing budget increased? Do you know how your customers have found out about your business?

5. What feedback have you received about your fees? Your way of doing business? Your personal style?

6. Who are your competitors? Where are they located? How do they promote themselves? How well known are they?

7. How well are your products doing in the marketplace? Is the demand increasing or declining? Is this change due to product quality, market fluctuations, or your own sales efforts?

8. What gaps in the marketplace could you fill in the future? What services can you offer that will set you apart from your competition?

9. Do you see a use for a product or service of yours that is not being exploited? Do you see a new market for one of your products or services?

If you monitor your business with the same fervor you apply to your personal investments, you will stay alert to opportunities for improvement. If you run a store, you may

try a variety of promotions to bring in new customers: newsletters, point-of-purchase displays, sales, discounts on certain products. But they will all be meaningless unless you can somehow relate the cost of the promotions to the resulting inquiries, sales, or increased foot traffic within your store.

We suggest that you sit down with an accountant, a business manager, and a promotions expert to see how the advice in this chapter can be customized to suit your business. They can help you set up a tracking system that can tell you, in a simple, easy way, how well your business is doing.

In business, half the battle is knowing who your customers are. The other half is reaching them and satisfying their needs. But that second half depends on the simple bookkeeping and the experimentation that help you reach a wider market in a clearer, more effective manner.

Other Areas to Monitor

Now that you have become sensitive to measuring results of your promotions, here are some other important aspects of your business to review periodically.

- *Operating expenses.* Are your expenses going up or remaining constant?
- *Employee productivity, morale, and performance.* Have you remained sensitive to what your employees want out of their jobs? Have they remained motivated?
- *Customer satisfaction.* Every now and then, you have to ask for feedback about your products and services. Maybe certain elements of your presentation are working against you. If you find out what people think, you can improve. If you ignore what they think, you risk the slow decline of your business.
- *Profitability, sales, gross, net revenues.* Is your business as profitable as it once was? Are you grossing more but

netting less? By keeping good records, you can find out what is causing this and take action to correct it.

- *The industry.* Is the demand for your product increasing or decreasing throughout the industry? What new trends and technologies must you keep up with to remain competitive?
- *Taxes and financial planning.* Are you earning more but not keeping any more? Is your financial and tax planning up to date with your increased income? If not, what are your future plans?

By holding a mirror up to your business, you see it the way it really is. You are forced to contemplate its weaknesses as well as its strengths. The same type of creative energy it took to launch your business will help you find the solutions to its problems.

CONCLUSION

It seems we have reached the place where you take over and begin writing the book of *your* escape, to offer your newly-acquired expertise to others looking to make it on their own!

We hope this book has carried you through to successful self-employment, or at least motivated you to begin the process that will lead you to the career you want.

Our experiences as self-employed individuals inspired us to write this book. We evaluated and reevaluated our own decisions. In these self-appraisals, we saw that our own moves into self-employment were, fortunately, right for us. Even the apparent drawbacks of self-employed status were positives in terms of personal growth and fulfillment. The challenges and difficulties of going it alone, once overcome or resolved, became victories and strengths.

In essence, *Out On Your Own*—because it relates to no specific field of employment—intends to foster the mindset and enthusiasm that the corporate employee needs to cross

the bridge to an autonomous career. We have tried to answer all of the questions and remove all of the uncertainties that the uncharted future of self-employment presents to corporate employees. More importantly, we have tried to demonstrate that *it can be done*.

So, to remain faithful to the positive state of mind—the *successful* state of mind—for which and with which we wrote this book, we wish good luck to all those entrepreneurial endeavors which are growing and developing in the minds of our readers, and especially to those endeavors which are taking place right now in the entrepreneurial world.

Index

About the Authors

Gary Blake, a former college professor, is the director of the Communication Workshop, a consulting firm helping business management improve writing and communication skills. His clients include the Chase Manhattan Bank, GAF, Lever Brothers, Maryland Casualty, and ITT.

His work has been published in such magazines as *Travel & Leisure, Harper's, Glamour, New York Times Book Review, Advertising Age,* and *New York.* Gary Blake is the author of *The Status Book* (Garden City, NY: Doubleday, 1978).

Robert W. Bly, a former corporate advertising manager, is an independent copywriter and consultant specializing in industrial and high-tech advertising. He has written copy for such companies as Brooklyn Union Gas, RCA, Grumman, Chemical Bank, Prentice-Hall, and Westinghouse.

He is the author of twelve books, including *Create the Perfect Sales Piece: A Do-It-Yourself Guide to Producing Brochures, Catalogs, Fliers, and Pamphlets* (New York: John Wiley & Sons, 1985). His articles have appeared in *Writer's Digest, Amtrak Express, Business Marketing, The Money Paper,* and *The Communicator's Journal.*